Writing with the authority of more than forty-five years of continuous experience of higher conscious states, GOPI KRISHNA has provided the world with a literal treasure of writings and discourses on the vast subjects of consciousness and evolution. During the last twenty years of his life, Gopi Krishna devoted his energies to presenting the world with his ideas about the present world condition and the future evolution of the human race. By the time he passed away in July 1984 at the age of 81, he was acclaimed as a leading authority on the science of Kundalini and Consciousness Research.

Gopi Krishna's quest was to bring awareness and understanding of the dangerous situation that mankind is in at present. He believed that the race is in a continuing state of evolution, but has now reached a crucial stage in this development. Mankind is on the verge of a giant leap toward higher states of consciousness but at the same time has the knowledge and means to destroy himself and the planet at the push of a button.

He asserts that there are Divine Laws which are ruling our progress. The time has now come for mankind to understand these inviolable Laws and learn to live in harmony with his fellow human beings so that our evolution may proceed in a healthy way.

Other Books by the Author
in UBSPD

1. Kundalini — The Secret of Yoga

2. The Purpose of Yoga

3. The Evolution of Higher Consciousness

4. Three Perspectives of Kundalini

5. The Wonder of the Brain

6. The Divine Possibilities in Man

— Ancient Secrets of
KUNDALINI
(Hidden in Panchastavi) —

Gopi Krishna

UBS Publishers' Distributors Pvt. Ltd.
5 Ansari Road, New Delhi-110 002
Phones: 3273601, 3266646 • Cable: ALLBOOKS • Fax: 3276593, 3274261
E-mail: ubspd@gobookshopping.com • Website: www.gobookshopping.com

10 First Main Road, Gandhi Nagar, Bangalore-560 009
Phones: 2253903, 2263901, 2263902 • Cable: ALLBOOKS
Fax: 2263904 • E-mail: ubspd.bng@bgl.vsnl.net.in

No. 60, Nelson Manickam Road, Chennai-600 029
Cable: UBSIPUB • E-mail: ubspd.che@md4.vsnl.net.in

8/1-B, Chowringhee Lane, Kolkata-700 016
Phones: 2441821, 2442910, 2449473 • Cable: UBSIPUBS
Fax: 2450027 • E-mail: ubspdcal@calvsnl.net.in

5 A, Rajendra Nagar, Patna-800 016
Phones: 672856, 673973, 686170 • Cable: UBSPUB • Fax: 686169
E-mail: ubspdpat1@sancharnet.in

80, Noronha Road, Cantonment, Kanpur-208 004
Phones: 369124, 362665, 357488 • Fax: 315122
E-mail: ubsknp@sancharnet.in

Distributors for Western India:
M/s Preface Books
Unit No. 223 (2nd floor), Cama Industrial Estate,
Sun Mill Compound, Lower Parel (W), Mumbai-400 013
Phone: 022-4988054 • Telefax: 022-4988048 • E-mail:
Preface@vsnl.com

Overseas Contact:
475 North Circular Road, Neasden, London NW2 7QG, UK
Tele: (020) 8450-8667 • Fax: (020) 8452 6612 Attn: UBS

© Gopi Krishna

First Published   1995
First Reprint   1996
Second Reprint   1997
Third Reprint   2002

Published in arrangement with
F.I.N.D. Research Trust
R.R. 5 Flesherton, Ontario, Canada, N0C 1E0

The Kundalini Research Foundation, Ltd.
P.O. Box 2248 Noroton Heights, CT. 06820, U.S.A.

Bioenergy Research Foundation
Carol L Strop CPA, 147 S Granados Avenue
Solana Beach, CA 92075, U.A.S.

Cover design: UBS Art Studio

Designed & Typeset at UBSPD in 11 pt. New Baskerville
Printed at Rajkamal Electric Press, Delhi

Contents

1. **Mystical Knowledge**   1
    The Antiquity of the Shakti Doctrines   1
    Kundalini in Other Cultures   11
    The Cosmic Life-Energy   21

2. **Shiva and Shakti**   30
    The Veil of Maya   30
    How Karma Works   34
    Normal and Paranormal Perception   38
    The Wonder of Higher Consciousness   47

3. **Mystical Experience and Modern Science**   58
    Mind and Brain   58
    Seven Levels of Consciousness   66
    Science and Indian Philosophy   77
    The Limitations of the Intellect   85

4. **The Nature of Reality**   94
    Mystical Vision — A Form of Genius   94
    True Mystical Experience   102
    Kundalini as the Creatrix   113
    Illuminative Radiance and a Cosmic Sound   119

5. **The Inner Universe**   127
    Altered States of Consciousness   127
    Perennial Ecstasy   134
    Kundalini as the Ideal of Beauty   142
    The Magnetic Power of the Illuminati   147

    References   155

    Panchastavi   157

1

Mystical Knowledge

THE ANTIQUITY OF THE SHAKTI DOCTRINES

*L*ike a priceless gem, lying hidden in the cavernous interior of a mountain, Panchastavi, a peerless hymn of praise addressed to Kundalini, has lain shielded from the eyes of the world by the snow-capped high mountain peaks that surround the beautiful vale of Kashmir, once said to be a lake known by the charming name of Sati-Sar. Except for one out of the five Cantos, which comprise the whole book, practically nothing is known about this superb composition, obviously of a Kashmiri poet to the erudite scholars in other parts of the country.

How such a rare book could remain unknown and unappreciated beyond the confines of the valley, for a period of over one thousand years, remains a mystery for which we have no explanation at present. Convulsive political upheavals and the barbarous oppression, through which the Brahmins of Kashmir passed for centuries, combined with the difficulties of communication and the isolated position of the valley, must have contributed a large share in relegating the work to the oblivion in which we find it at present. This is not true of Panchastavi alone. There are other matchless gems of literature relating to the Shaiva doctrines, peculiar to Kashmir, and excellent Sufi compositions which still await translation into a world-language to contribute their share to the literary treasures shared in common by all mankind.

The only other work in the whole gamut of Shakti Shastra in India comparable to Panchastavi is the famous work, known as *Saundarya Lahari*, attributed by some scholars to the far-famed mystic-philosopher Shankaracharya who, it is said, flourished in the 8th century A.D. The issue of authorship of the said work has not been finally settled yet and the position is contested by other writers. Saundarya Lahari is divided into two parts. The first part, known as Ananda Lahari, or the Wave of Bliss, consists of 41 verses and the second, which is of 62 verses, is known as Saundarya Lahari proper, meaning the Wave of Beauty. The two together make a total of 103 slokas. There is conflict of views about the number of verses also. The esteem and importance in which this book has been held can be readily assessed from the fact that no less than thirty-six well-known commentaries have been written on it, and almost every syllable has been made the theme of lengthy discussions by the learned commentators.

The commentaries, though not radically different from one another, often present divergent views and theories and attempt diverse interpretations of the hymns in keeping with them. Shankaracharya is said to have based Ananda Lahari on another famous work, *Subhagodaya*, ascribed to the guru of his guru, known by the name of Gaudapada. It is, in fact, considered to be only an extension of the latter. This little detail has been given to show the close kinship between the philosophy of Vedanta, as expounded by Shankara, and Shri Vidya or the doctrine of Cosmic Energy which forms the basis of the Tantric tradition.

There are striking similarities between Panchastavi and Saundarya Lahari. Some of the views expressed are identical and even the expression is, at places, somewhat similar. The wealth of knowledge and the depth of observation displayed, combined with the beauty of poetic expression and the use of appropriate words and phrases, are so remarkable that it is no wonder that the authorship of Saundarya Lahari, at least, has been attributed to Lord Shiva Himself, and Shankaracharya is said to have been only the *Mantra-drashta* or *Rishi*, which means the work was revealed to him.

The same revelational origin can be ascribed to Panchastavi also. Its authorship is shrouded in mystery, but there can be no doubt that it is the inspired composition of a yogi who had reached the highest stage of realization. The work has been cited as a source book by several eminent scholars of Kashmir, but the name of the author has always remained undisclosed. Without revealing his identity, the author has referred to himself in very humble terms in some of the verses and in one definitely acknowledged his unrepayable debt to the Goddess for all the blessings of this world that had enriched his life.

Commenting on the authorship and date of composition of Panchastavi, Professor K.N. Dhar writes:

"In some manuscripts in the Kashmir Government Research Library the name of the author has been given as Laghavacharya and in some as Acharya Prithvidhara, a disciple of Shambunatha. In one manuscript the name of the poet has been written as Shri Ramchandracharya. Kashmiri tradition even ascribes the work to Abhinavagupta. In verses from Panchastavi quoted by the commentators of *Vidyarnava* and *Saubhagya Ratnakara* the author has been mentioned as Dharmacharya. Nityananda, the commentator of *Tripura-Mahima-Stotra,* corroborates this view. In our own time, Harabhatta Shastri has also taken Dharmacharya to be the author of Panchastavi.

"The very fact that there is no unanimity of opinion about the authorship of Panchastavi lends to the conclusion that actually the author himself chose to remain anonymous. The last verse of the first chapter seems to subscribe to this view. The use of *laghustvatmani* (insignificance of his own self) debars him from proclaiming his name. This denotes the highest degree of humility. Hitopadesha acclaims Knowledge as the bestower of humility. As to the names Acharya, Kalidasa, and Dharmacharya, it can be said that actually these are not proper names but only titles. *Acharya* means a preceptor and *Dharmacharya* means a preceptor of dharma; here obviously Shaiva dharma is meant. At times even scribes, when not aware of the name of an author, themselves put in a fictitious or titular name in place of the actual writer. We are, therefore, forced to conclude that the authorship of Panchmastavi is still an unsolved mystery.

"Panchastavi contains in it the quintessence of the Tantric nondualism. The earliest extant reference to it is found in the *Saraswati Kanthabharna* of King Bhoja. The probable date of composition of *Saraswati Kanthabharna* is between 1030 and 1050 A.D. Hence Panchastavi must have been composed much earlier than it for the reason that by the time of Bhoja its poetic merit must have been established on a firm footing as only then could it deserve a place in a work on poetics.

"Saundarya Lahari, ascribed to Shankaracharya, can be said to be a sister volume to Panchastavi. For this reason, Lakshmidhara in his commentary on the former has quoted profusely from it. It is very difficult to say which composition of the two is earlier, what debt they owe to each other and what the common source behind the two is. It can be said, however, without fear of contradiction that the subject-matter of these two compositions being similar, as also the phrase and idiom at many places, it is possible both might have been composed simultaneously . . . . It is said that

Shankaracharya became a Shakti worshiper during his sojourn in Kashmir.[1] Local tradition of Kashmir confirms this view. Shankara's dates have been fixed between 788 and 830 A.D.,[2] so it seems probable that Panchastavi was also composed during this period.

"If it is argued that Panchastavi is posterior to Saundarya Lahari, still it could not have been composed after 1030 to 1050 A.D. In any case, the upper limit can be fixed at 788 to 820 A.D. (Shankara's visit to Kashmir and the composing of Saundarya Lahari by him), and the lower limit by the date of Bhoja's treatise on poetics (*Saraswati Kanthabharna*, i.e. 1030 to 1050 A.D.). In fairness to the author, it can be concluded that Panchastavi must have been composed in the latter half of the 9th century and by the time of Bhoja, its verses must have attained a high degree of fame."[3]

According to Tantric concepts, the ultimate reality (Sada-Shiva) manifests itself in a dual role as consciousness, or the subject, and as energy, translated into the visible universe. As consciousness, He is masculine and as energy feminine and, therefore, is designated as *Ardha-Narishware*. This concept of the totality of existence, as partly male and partly female, is represented in Chinese cosmogony by the terms yin and yang, in the Samkhya system of philosophy by Purusha and Prakriti, in the Hindu pantheon by Vishnu and Lakshmi, Rudra and Rudrani, Shiva and Parvati, Brahma and Saraswati, and in the Vaishnavite cult of India as Krishna and Radha or Rama and Sita. In the Assyrian, Babylonian and Egyptian theophany, this combination is designated by the names of Tammuz and Ishtar or Isis, and we find their counterparts in the old Greek and Roman religions also. It is thus evident that the belief in a dual aspect of the Creator and the Created has been very widespread in the past and can be traced even to prehistoric primitive beliefs and myths.

The sexual division of living creatures into male and female, and the irresistible attraction that one sex has for the other could not but impress the primitive mind with the idea that what it witnessed in created beings must also apply to the supernatural forces or Gods responsible for the creation. It goes without question that there must be a profound ontological significance attached to this sexual division of living creatures into male and female. What lies behind this mystery is yet unintelligible to us. The purpose of propagation could be fulfilled in other ways also. It was not necessary for the continuation of life forms that they should be bisexual, each sex needing the other for the fulfillment of the reproductive impulse.

The primary forms of life propagated themselves by division — one cell divided into two, two into four and so on. The cellular organizations of all animals and plants grow by the primordial process of cell division. The same phenomenon is repeated in the womb after conception. The ultimate product of this process of rapid cell multiplication resolves itself either as a female or male, by a mysterious impulse present in the fertilized ovum, or in both the parent cells, influenced this way or that by the method of their combination. This finished product, emerging as a male or a female, through a most powerful unaccountable urge that reaches down to the very depths of one's being, finds itself drawn to its opposite with a magnetic force, as if the two parts belonged to one stream of being, and had been torn apart to hunger for each other till they combined into one again. The whole process of love and sexual union in which the two participants unite not only their bodies, but even merge their individualities and, in the excess of emotion, wish to become one with the whole being of the other, is a testimony to this compulsion.

This polarity of male and female, active and passive, penetrates not only to the deepest levels of the human organism, but also to the deepest layers of matter also. The nucleus and the remaining mass of protoplasm in each living cell, the active and passive or excitory and inhibitory nerve currents flowing through the sympathetic and parasympathetic nervous systems, the active and passive character of the cerebral hemispheres, the attraction and repulsion in the atoms of matter, the positively and negatively charged constituents of the atom, or the positive and negative forms of electricity are all indications of this bipolarity in the basic substance of all created objects. Further investigation may even trace this polarity to those highly diffused and still undetermined levels of matter from which the nebular systems and the stellar universes originate. In fact, the very fundamental movements in the invisible medium from which the material universe is born might be the result of a commotion caused by the union of two extremely subtle complementary forces, like the ferment caused by the coming together of the male and the female for the purpose of procreation.

Who knows that the microcosmic drama of love, enacted by man and woman on the miniature stage of the earth, might be the diminutive replica of the macrocosmic play enacted by the primary gigantic forces of creation —an Infinite Giant Consciousness and its unbounded Energy — designated as Shiva and Shakti in the Tantric lore of India. There is nothing so mysterious and surprising in the universe as consciousness. The tiny, flickering flame of awareness in each of us which seems so weak and vacillating in embodied life, once released from the prisonhouse of senses, becomes a colossus — the predominant Reality of the universe which no power can overcome, no force dominate or destroy. We seldom experience it in its macrocosmic form and, hence, are not able, except rarely, to understand its mystery.

According to the Tantras, there is a female and male principle in every human being, something far more profound and fundamental than the *anima* and *animus* of Jungian psychology. The male principle is designated by a point (*bindu*) in the crown of the head, and the female principle by a triangle (*trikona*) — emblematic of the female organ of generation — close to the base of the spine where Kundalini lies asleep, coiled three and a half times, closing the aperture leading to *Brahma-randhra* or the cavity of Brahma in the head. Her awakening implies the upward flow of the energy used for reproduction to unite with the conscious principle or *bindu* in the head. In other words, consciousness and its creative Energy, which are bifurcated in us in the 'knower' and his 'Creative Power' come together again to illuminate the almighty, limitless nature of the former.

Considered from the biological angle, the arousal of Kundalini implies the commencement of a new metabolic activity at the base of the spine in which the entire reproductive system with its blood vessels, arteries, veins, nerves and other tissues is deeply involved. The general impression prevailing that Kundalini can be awakened to activity merely with certain practices of Hatha-Yoga, like concentration, *pranayama* or *bandhas* is not correct. If it were so, then everyone who doggedly persisted in these disciplines long enough could win in the enterprise. But the hard fact that only a few succeed in an age presents an enigma to which those who pose as accomplished teachers of the science have no answer except to lay the failure at the door of karma of the disciple.

The statements like "She should be led as a rider leads a horse," or that "She should be despoiled by force," contained in treatises on Hatha-Yoga, are also not based on a correct appreciation of the position. It is obvious that some of the authors of Yoga manuals are mere professional teachers, as far away from illumination as their lay disciples. It is important to bear this fact always in mind in drawing inferences about spiritual matters. There is a world of difference between the inspired compositions of the illuminati and the labored production of the professional and the erudite. The only possible effect of all the yogic exercises and disciplines, however strenuous or complex they might be, is to stimulate or coax the dormant power to activity by this means or that. But whether the stimulation would have the desired effect of generating the metabolic processes, which result in the circulation of a new form of nerve energy in the body and the flow of the reproductive secretions into the various organs and the brain, leading to a new pattern of consciousness, is a different matter altogether.

There are many people who, while practicing sundry forms of meditation with or without *pranayama* or other exercises, peculiar to Hatha-Yoga, experience various kinds of sensations in the region of Kundalini or *kanda*, commencing a little below the navel to the perineum, both in front or behind. These sensations range from mere throbbing or the feeling of a current moving upward to a pleasurable tickling or erotic itching in the reproductive region with intermittent flashes of light of various hues in the head. All these sensations and impressions of light, if real, and not the creations of fancy in suggestible individuals can be definitely traced to the stimulation of the Serpent Power. They are not, however, indicative of sustained activity of the mechanism which is absolutely necessary for the working of processes leading to the transformation of consciousness.

According to the classical manuals of Hatha-Yoga, the *sadhaka* is enjoined in his daily practice to imagine the whole process of arousal of the Divine Power from Muladhara, the root center at the base of the spine, to *Brahma-randhra*, the twelve-petalled lotus behind the roof of the palate, passing through all the six lotuses on the cerebrospinal axis that lie in the way. The visualization is to be done according to descriptions furnished by the preceptor about the formation of the lotuses, their color, number of petals, the letters of the alphabet shown on each petal and other accessories, as also on the nature of the Divine Energy itself. She has to be fancied like a flash of lightning, with the brilliance of thousands of suns, pouring into the brain with the milky-white lustre of the moon, assuming divergent colors at different places, as for instance, the hues of a rainbow in the forehead, the radiance of the sun in the heart, appearing like a vermilion-colored lotus fibre on Her passage through the innermost sheath (*Brahma-nadi*) of the spinal cord. The practitioner has also to concentrate on the sounds that occur on the arousal of the Power, like the music made by a swarm of bees in flight or a distant waterfall, a conch, a murmuring stream, far-off tinkling of bells or an endlessly prolonged nasal 'Aum'.

In this age of lightning speed and ideas of easy achievement applied to almost all undertakings, including even enlightenment, it is extremely difficult to imagine the life of an anchorite who set himself to the formidable task of arousing the Serpent Power in the past. Day and night, with only brief intervals for meals and other basic necessities of life, he consecrated himself in lonely hermitages and ashrams to the enterprise, undergoing various practices and disciplines, some of them extremely dangerous and painful, without any thought to the world, to bodily injury, mental derangement or even death. Years and even the whole life passed in this way, with this one aim before his mental horizon, indifferent to the body and physical comfort, until his prime was spent without in the least realizing the dream. This happens even now and millions of ascetics in India pass lives of extreme austerity and hard labor to the end without ever attaining the beatific state. Since the awakening of the Power depends on a host of biological factors, one of the most important of which is favorable heredity, it can be safely assumed that a large proportion of the aspirants have to rest content either with bodily sensations, resembling those of the actual awakening, random flashes of light, or dream-like visionary experiences, partly real and partly imaginary, evoked by their constant preoccupation with the subject.

We see this actually happening in the case of contemporary seekers who devote themselves to various religious practices and disciplines in our own time. Among the millions upon millions of people who take to various kinds of Yoga or other meditational practices, there is a general tendency to attach an exaggerated importance to the subjective signs as, for instance, flashes of light before the eyes, sounds in the ears or sensations felt in various parts of the body, under the impression that they are the harbingers of success in the undertaking. This sort of wishful thinking has, not unoften, the very reverse effect of enlarging the ego and inculcating ideas of self-importance. The only sure signs of enlightened consciousness are inner illumination, inspired thought and diction, abounding love, humility and an altered perception of the objective world.

The reason for this commonly-met, erroneous frame of mind is that the biological aspect of the disciplines is often entirely overlooked. Once the psychosomatic nature of the Power Reservoir of Kundalini is clearly understood, the whole concept of religion and the transcendental will undergo a radical change, and all the signs and symptoms that attend the practice of Yoga or other religious disciplines will be evaluated in the context of their biological impact on the organism and not merely on the basis of the subjective performance. What the author of Panchastavi ascribes to the Shakti is the everyday experience of the accomplished yogi. The same experience, with minor variations, is repeated in hundreds, even thousands, of inspired compositions of the illuminati of India born in different parts of the country.

KUNDALINI IN OTHER CULTURES

The mechanism of the human body is so constituted that the individual has no control over its involuntary or autonomous functions and is often as unconcerned about what transpires in his own interior as he is of what happens in the bowels of the earth. Sometimes the infinitely varied activity of his mortal frame — the flow of blood, the pumping of the heart, the working of the stomach, liver or the intestines — is sharply brought to his notice in an attack of illness, when something goes wrong in the system, and he writhes in pain until normalcy is restored and a lid is dropped over these disturbances again. This happens somewhat in the same way as an earthquake brings the ever-fluctuating nature of the fiery interior of the earth to our notice now and then to be forgotten as soon as the tremors are over. We have no knowledge whatsoever how the flame of our surface consciousness with all its individuality, extensive memory and intellectual acumen is kept alight by the combined activity of our organs and cells and what incredibly accurate mechanism maintains the extremely delicate balance of hormones and other complex chemical compounds in our system.

The complexity of the body and the intricate nature of each part, organ, gland and their tissues defy description. The harmonious way in which countless millions of differently constituted cells and hundreds of organs and their parts work together, as one harmonious whole, is a miracle of efficiency and order. The brain is the most marvelous part of this intricate machine, full of wonder from the single cell to the most complex organization contained in it. "Our intelligence can no more realize the immensity of the brain than the extent of the sidereal universe," says Dr. Alexis Carrell. "The cerebral substance contains more than twelve thousand millions of cells. These cells are connected with one another by fibrils, and each fibril possesses several branches. By means of these fibrils they associate several billions of times. And this crowd of tiny individuals and invisible fibrils, despite its undreamed-of complexity, works as if it were essentially one. To observers accustomed to the simplicity of the molecular and atomic worlds, the brain appears as an unintelligible and marvelous phenomenon."[4]

In a delicate machine so intricate and sensitive as the human body, in the whole as also in all its components, how can all the supernormal and bizarre phenomena, associated with Kundalini, occur without drastically changing its rhythm or causing disorder in its normal working in one way or the other? The point to be remembered here is that the awakening of Kundalini is an activity for which a provision already exists in the human frame, in the same way as there exists a provision in the body of a woman for conception and the bearing of a child. However strange or bizarre the manifestations might be they are then the offshoots of a development for which the organism already stands equipped, as a result of natural processes about which we are still in the dark. But if no such provision exists, and the body is forced to a type of activity for which there is no sanction from nature, then it means that any attempt to arouse the Power can only lead to unnatural conditions for which human beings are not genetically designed.

This is an important issue which needs empirical investigation for its solution one way or the other. If the hoary concept of Kundalini has a basis in reality then all that is claimed for it, in Panchastavi and in other classical documents, must be verifiable by experiment. Both in the case of the universe and our own bodies we see the rule of order, from the atoms to the suns and from the single cell to the whole organism. A slight pain or grief starts a chain reaction in our system of which we generally never know the whole extent. It is, therefore, inconceivable that the sudden release of a power which can drastically alter the activity of the brain and raise consciousness to entirely undreamed-of heights can have no impact on the organism and leave no impression on the brain cells or other organs and tissues forming it. If there is no appreciable effect on the body, it means that the whole phenomenon — the lights seen, the voices heard, the joy experienced, the knowledge gained, the wisdom acquired and the contact with Divinity experienced— are all purely mental or spiritual occurrences without any relation to the physical frame of man. In such a case the objective verification of the phenomenon can never be possible and the investigators will always continue to be in doubt about whether the condition is purely imaginary and delusive or signifies the supersensory perception of a Reality that we have no other means to know.

This is not all. If the experiences undergone in the new, altered state of consciousness cause no reaction in the brain and no impact on the body, it would mean that the condition is merely an artificial state brought about by our own efforts and not a natural target for which there already exists a provision in the psychosomatic endowment of human beings. Then the doctrine of reincarnation loses its purpose and the ideas of divinity associated with such experiences all their weight. Then there will also arise the question whether the practices and disciplines of the kind that lead to this extraordinary subjective state and, in fact, the whole sphere of religion itself, are at all conducive to human welfare. Because if the experience has no natural sanction behind it on account of its total dissociation with biological factors and the normal mental condition of man, how can we know that it would not have an unnatural and unhealthy effect in the long run both on the individual and the race?

There is no doubt that in one form or the other the secret of Kundalini was known in many parts of the world even in prehistoric times. There are unmistakable indications to show that the basic principles of Tantric Yoga must have been known to the populations of the Indus Valley civilization which flourished from about 3,000 to 1,500 B.C. The high grade of civilization reached, with its planned towns, broad, regularly aligned streets, public wells, lampposts, sentry boxes, elaborate drainage systems, spacious public baths, vast granaries, pillared halls, beautifully painted pottery, high-class furniture, high-quality weapons and implements of bronze and copper, artistically made toys for the children, jewelry and ornaments, and accurate weights and measures, all testify to a standard of living almost as high as of the still developing countries in modern times. Bullock carts in use then, more than 4,500 years ago, still ply with but little change in design in many parts of India today.

It is not, therefore, surprising that people with such a sophisticated urban life, persisting for no less than 1,500 years, should be deeply interested in the mystery of life and death. It can well be that in their ardent search for an answer to the riddle they might have stumbled on the secret of Kundalini or learnt it from an anterior civilization. When we once divest religion and religious experience from the supernatural and miraculous and treat it as an inherent impulse in the psychoso matic organism of man, drawing him towards a higher life of the spirit, we then also have to admit that the said impulse must gather in strength and lead to intense efforts to solve the mystery every time, when the ecological factors are favorable to its growth. It is a great error to undervalue the great contribution of the ancient world to the science of life. What is needed is a knowledge of the key to the religious hieroglyphics of the past. When this key, lost in the labyrinth of mysteries, magic and alchemy is found, it will not be difficult to find the central path which, by turning and twisting upon itself, has formed a baffling maze and now appears impossible to pick out.

One of the most remarkable finds of the Indus Valley civilization is a seal bearing the figure of a three-faced deity, sitting in Yoga posture with an erect organ of generation, surrounded by a number of animals such as a tiger, a buffalo and a rhinoceros, with a deerskin under the seat. This is obviously a representation of the God Shiva who is said to be three-faced and is also called Pashupati, or Lord of Animals. Our inability to decipher the Indus Valley script keeps the religious beliefs of the people still shrouded in darkness. Besides this clear representation of God Shiva, there are also a number of semi-nude figures of Goddesses on other seals. Some of them depict scenes of human and animal sacrifice. It is obvious that a form of worship, analogous to the Shiva-Shakti cults of India of our own day, was in vogue among the people of the vanished civilization. This is confirmed by the discovery of conical and cylindrical stones which can only be regarded as phallic symbols or *lingas*, and also small stones representative of the female organ of generation, or *yonis*. We have thus no doubt that the cult of Kundalini, with its emphasis on the male and female organs of generation, and their symbolic representation, both in the outer and inner modes of worship, was known to the denizens of the Indus Valley. It is also very possible that the evolution of their high quality of civilization might have been due, to a large extent, to the voluntary cultivation of higher mental faculties by the arousal of Kundalini among the spiritual hierarchy that dominated the populations. With the decipherment of the obscure script a flood of light is likely to be thrown on the religious beliefs and practices of these people which will bring interesting facts about the Serpent Power known to them to the forefront. Broadly speaking, from the material provided by the seals and other relics, there can hardly be any dispute about the fact that a system of worship and ritual, akin to the Tantric system and Yoga, was prevalent in India long before the advent of the Aryans about 2,000 years before the birth of Christ.

A stone torso from Harappa is hyphallic. Seals inscribed with a bull pictograph, similar to some excavated from the Indus Valley sites, have been found on the islands of Bahrain and Failaka in the Persian Gulf. There must have existed a lively intercourse in trade and culture between the people of the Indus Valley and those of Mesopotamia and Egypt. In the Sanctuary of Sanctuaries in the Temple at Karnak, there is a row of male figures with erect phallus, a clear symbol of Kundalini. The figure is of *khem* which means the erectile force, also called Amso Horus, meaning erect phallus.

Each of these civilizations had, however, its own characteristics:

"Most of the seals (of the Indus Valley) bear also a short

inscription in pictographic script," says Sir Mortimer Wheeler, "which, in spite of brave attempts, has not been interpreted. The pictographs are as different from those of Mesopotamia and Egypt as these are from each other. It is an interesting phenomenon that, within a short range of time and space, three great civilizations produced three utterly divergent systems of notation."[5]

The belief in the existence of a feminine natural force, the source of fertility, generative power, longevity, knowledge, inspiration, prosperity, manifestation of the divine, and the like, has been very widespread from the remotest past. It is noteworthy that the worship of this Divine power under various forms, intimately connected with mysteries and myths, was widely prevalent in all the vanished civilizations of which any record has been left. There is a parallelism between the Shakti of Panchastavi and the Ishtar of Assyrio-Babylonian culture which is not a little surprising. Ishtar is the spouse of Tammuz who is variously described as hunter, herdsman, Sun-God, God of Righteousness, God of Fertility, etc.

God Shiva, too, is depicted as a hunter. "O Shavari, the wife of the hunter Shiva," says Panchastavi (IV.15), "bearing the crest of peacock feathers on Thy head, with curly locks of soft, shining, deep brown hair, a rosary of red berries resting on Thy heavy breasts, in color like the evening sky, with a face like red coral and soft and tender hands, O Thou Shakti of Shankara (Shiva) I bow down before Thee." Again in verse 3 of canto V it says, "Thou, garbed as a huntress (Shavari), followed Shiva, clever in his role as a hunter, to afford protection to Arjuna. My obeisance to Thee again and again." In some ancient inscriptions Tammuz is bracketed with Shams, signifying the Sun-God. Shiva is also the Soul-illuminating Sun-God Savitar, invoked in the Gayatri Mantra, and Kundalini is Savitri, his spouse. Shams has two attendants — Kettu and Mesaru. Rahu and Kettu are two demons who cause the eclipse of the sun, according to Indian mythology.

Some of the legends relating to Tammuz as an Assyrian and Babylonian God date back to 4,000 years before the birth of Christ. It was held that as the Sun-God he passed the six months between the beginning of autumn and end of winter in the underworld. Compare this with verse 9 of canto IV of Panchastavi in which it is said: — "For One like Shiva, dressed in skins, His body besmeared with ash from (cremated) dead bodies, wandering for alms, dancing in the habitations of ghosts, and gathering hosts of earth-spirits round Himself, it is only Thy association with Him that lends charm to all these attributes." Again, one of the names of Shiva is Pashupati, Lord of Beasts, in which form he is shown on one of the ancient seals of the Indus culture, Tammuz is a herdsman and shepherd, caretaker of flocks of sheep and herds of animals. Krishna's boyhood is spent as a cowherd and he delights in the company of cowherd boys and girls.

In other inscriptions Ishtar is referred to as Zarpanit, the consort of Marduk, the chief god of the Babylonians. This name in Sumer signified the "silver shining", and later was interpreted by Semites to mean "seed producing", both terms which are applicable to Shakti (Kundalini) also. She was said to be the "Creatrix of all creatures," and also called Ishtar of Wisdom. Among the birds the dove was especially sacred to her, probably because of its erotic temperament. In a hymn she is entitled as the "glad-eyed Goddess of Desire" and in another hymn as "the amorous Mother-Goddess at whose side no god draweth near." At another place she is called "a loving courtesan," and in this respect is depicted with emphasized sexual features.

In a hymn she says, "I turn the male to the female, I turn the female to the male." She is the awakener of sexual impulse in both human beings and animals, and the cause of sexual union. According to Herodotus she was called Mylitta at Babylon which signified "she who causes to bear." In her list of titles she is termed as "the opener of the loins," as "the Mother of Gods," and as "Creatress of mankind who causes all created things to flourish." She was regarded as the mistress of magical arts with which she counteracted the evil designs of demons. She is also the "queen of all dwelling places," imparting all Laws, "wearing the ruler's crown." She is the inspirer of prophets and the source of their messages, also the causer of revelations and the power behind the oracles.

With all her life-giving properties Ishtar is also the Goddess of Destruction, the Storm-Goddess and the Goddess of War. "She is the lofty one who causes the heavens to tremble, the earth to quake, the fire to rage, who causes the bird-like Zu (the storm cloud) to fly from the house, who casts down mountains like dead bodies." In art she was often represented holding a caduceus of two serpents. As early as the time of Hammurabi, she was shown in a triad with the moon and sun. Sun, moon and Ishtar of the Babylonian cult corresponds to the sun, moon and fire (*pingala, ida* and *sushumna*) of the Tantras. She is also depicted as the morning and evening star, Venus. In a hymn she says, "Ishtar, the goddess of the morning and Ishtar, the goddess of the evening am I." Ishtar seems to have been the most important divinity of the Assyrio-Babylonian pantheon. She absorbed so many other goddesses and exercised such a variety of functions that she became almost the supreme divinity.

Can there be any two opinions about the issue whether Ishtar of the Assyrio-Babylonian pantheon, wedded to the Sun-God who is also a hunter, herdsman and the god of the nether world, of ghosts and goblins, has a clearly marked identity with the Mother Goddess of the Indus Valley, shown semi-nude on some of the seals? She was later called Shakti, the consort of Pashupati, Lord of the Beasts, sitting in Yoga posture obviously in a state of *samadhi,* with *urdhava-linga* or an erect organ of generation. Lord Shiva is said to be *urdhava-retas* (with upward directed reproductive energy) and *urdhava-linga* (with erect phallus) both. The undeniably biological aspect of the cult is in this way brought into unmistakable prominence. There is every reason to suppose that the other attributes of Ishtar, mentioned in the Babylonian records, myths and legends or depicted in art, must also be similar or approximately so to the Mother Goddess of the Indus Valley. She is the Goddess of love, fecundity, learning and arts, the morning and evening star, the source of revelation and occult knowledge, of inspired speech and prophecy, also the Goddess of prosperity and success, and the Creatrix of all beings. What is more relevant to our theme is that she is often depicted holding a caduceus in her hand, an unmistakable sign of Kundalini.

When we see how Shakti or Kundalini is depicted in Panchastavi and other ancient manuals, practically no doubt is left about her identity with Ishtar. She is Durga, the benign Creatrix of all animate and inanimate objects, Chandi, the fierce War-Goddess, armed with sword, spear, discus, the goad, etc., resembling the well-armed Ishtar and spreads destruction among the Asuras (demons). She is Saraswati, the Goddess of Learning and Wisdom, the source of inspiration and eloquence, the dispenser of psychic powers and magical gifts, as also the Goddess of Destruction and natural calamities. She wears a crest of peacock feathers on her head. In some depictions Ishtar is also shown with a feathery crest. Like her, Ishtar also resembles the sky. Verse 18 of canto IV of Panchastavi makes the similarity so striking that the two appear to be different names of the same divine entity. "O Bhagvati (Sovereign of the Universe)," it says, "though in Thy transcendental aspect Thou art one without a second (the position of the Supreme Deity allotted to Ishtar), yet Thou art the daughter of Prajapati (Lord of the Universe), also the serpentine Kundalini, dweller in the cavity of the heart, as also Katyayani (dressed in red), also Kamla (Lakshmi, the Goddess of Wealth) and Kalavati (the Goddess of Arts), in this way verily, like a dancing girl, Thou art seen in countless forms (and roles)." Ishtar is depicted as a courtesan and also as the Goddess of Prosperity and Art.

THE COSMIC LIFE-ENERGY

In trying to assign a chronological order for the ideas expressed in the Agama scriptures and Shakti Shastras, including Panchastavi, we are confronted by the amazing position that the concept of a divine feminine Power that can grant wisdom, inspiration, magical skill, artistic talent and prophecy, who is wedded to the Sun-God (Savitar), is very old, older perhaps than the Assyrio-Egyptian cultures which flourished more than 4,000 years before the birth of Christ. The age assigned to the Vedas, the oldest written religious scriptures in the world, according to most scholars, does not exceed this period up to date. In the Vedas, too, she is referred to as Usha (the dawn), Saraswati (the Goddess of Learning and Art), Prithvi (the Mother Earth, wedded to Father Heavens), and alluded to in several verses as Dyavaprithvi. The famous Gayatri Mantra of the Rig Veda definitely refers to Kundalini as the source of spiritual and mental illumination. "May we attain the glorious light of the god Savitar," says the Mantra, "May He inspire our prayers." Savitar is not merely the Sun-God, but something more than the mundane orb of light, namely the Divine Power behind it. Savitar enlightens the world and awakens immortality.

"No good and sufficient explanation of the peculiar sanctity attached to this verse (the Gayatri Mantra) has ever been given," says Colebrook. "It is not made remarkable either by thought or diction among many other Vedic verses of similar tenor."[6] Gayatri Mantra is said to be the quintessence of the Vedas and the highest Mantra of all because Gayatri as Kundalini embodies the most profound mystery of human existence; because the whole teaching of the Vedas revolves round this one supreme secret of nature. Colebrook's comment is occasioned as the esoteric significance of the Mantra has not been understood, and because the biological mechanism of illumination, providing the one and only pathway to reach the intelligent forces of creation, is still a closed book to scholars and scientists.

From immemorial times Gayatri Mantra has been breathed into the ear of the disciple by the guru at the time of the investiture ceremony of the Sacred Thread, marking the commencement of the *Brahmachari ashram* (period of discipleship) among the three twice-born castes of the Hindus. The investiture is done using a triple thread with a knot tied by the guru (representing the three channels *ida*, *pingala* and *sushumna*, with a hard-to-pierce knot at the navel, heart and *ajna* chakras). The thread is worn by the initiate round the neck from the left shoulder and hanging on the right side below the arm. Now, in this age of vastly extended knowledge, with its emphasis more on the material than the spiritual side, little do the gurus, who perform the ceremony, and their disciples who undergo the initiation, know that they are both participants in a function which, without their being aware of it, centers round one of the most jealously guarded secrets of nature, known from remotest antiquity but never grasped in all its significance to this day.

Gayatri Mantra represents the cream of the Vedas, because it is the Wish-Fulfilling Tree of Paradise and can bestow all the ardently sought-after boons dear to the heart of every mortal — longevity, bodily strength, intellectual preeminence, genius, psychic gifts and, last of all, the glorious crown of human life, the knowledge of Self. Savitri is the same as Gayatri, namely the power invoked in the hymn to Savitar in the Rig Veda. It is in this sense of Gayatri or Kundalini that She has been apostrophized in Saundarya Lahari. Parvati, the spouse of Shiva, is also known as Savitri. On the other hand, Shiva is known as Gayatri-Vallabh, the beloved of Gayatri. This clearly signifies that Gayatri is the same as Parvati, daughter of the mountain (or the Mountain-Goddess of antiquity) and also the same as Savitri. There can be no dispute over the fact that, even according to the Vedic connotation, the word Gayatri signifies the Cosmic Life-

Energy or Kundalini. The seeds of the Tantric concepts are, therefore, deeply embedded in the Vedas. The distinction between the Vedic Gayatri and the Tantric Gayatri, alluded to by Arthur Avalon in his *Introduction to Tantra Shastra*, is merely semantic. In actual fact, in both the Vedic and Tantric forms of *sadhana* Gayatri is identical with and signifies Kundalini, the Divine Energy leading to inner illumination. Like a live electric wire, twisted into innumerable loops and folds, each outwardly entirely dissimilar to the other yet charged with the same current, all religions, creeds and sects of mankind, all secret methods of mind-training, magic or sorcery and all disciplines for the attainment of mystical ecstasy or religious beatitude, which ever led to some tangible result, one and all had their roots in Kundalini. There is no doubt that what I am asserting was known in almost all the vanished civilizations of the past. The basis of all the mysteries, whether Babylonian, Egyptian or Greek, can be definitely traced to Kundalini. We shall discuss this issue a little more in detail in another volume. Here it is sufficient to mention that the worship of the feminine force of nature, of the phallus and the female organ of generation, stretching to remote periods of time, had its origin in the instinctive recognition by the ancients of the bilateral activity of the reproductive mechanism, leading to procreation on the one side and to mental and spiritual evolution on the other.

The naive explanation of scholars that phallus worship is the outcome of primitive superstition about fertility and birth is itself the product of scientific superstition of the nineteenth century. The Indian tradition of Kundalini has an empirical background of more than three thousand years, supported by the testimony of disciplined savants whose veracity is beyond question. The current research on consciousness and psi phenomena would reveal one day how far in advance they have been to the modern savants of the science of life. We are now able to formulate this conclusion on account of the vast increase in the knowledge of the human organism that has occurred in recent times. But for this recognition the obscurity attending the origin of the religious impulse would never cease to exist.

In order to assess the importance of Panchastavi and, in fact, of all the Tantric literature in general, it is necessary to dwell briefly on the inevitable manifold impact of the knowledge of Kundalini on all spheres of human life, once the existence of this powerhouse is empirically established. The first outcome of the research would be the emergence of a new Super-Science dealing with mind and consciousness. Through this science the present highly-developed human intellect would gain the first insights into the now totally hidden universe of consciousness. This would lead to staggering revelations beyond anything known to or conceived of by science at present.

The power behind life is incomprehensible to the human intellect. The attitude of adoration, submission, surrender, wonder and mystification, evinced throughout in Panchastavi and other works on Shri Vidya (the science of Cosmic Life-Energy), is the outcome of this incomprehensible nature of Shakti. The universe of matter, intelligible to us through our intellect, is but one compartment of a creation infinite in its variety and the forces and elements involved. Matter is one, Cosmic Life-Energy is another. There might be varied patterns of Cosmic Life-Energy operating on other planets and in other regions of the universe, entirely different from the Life-Energy operating on earth. There might be other forces of which we have no perception or knowledge active in other areas of the cosmos. We see only what is revealed to us by our five senses and the mind. No instrument ever fashioned can bring to us perception of a force, substance or entity beyond the cognitive power of our mind.

The transformation of consciousness, brought about by the arousal of Kundalini, introduces a new element into our field of perception. The world of mind, imperceptible before, becomes cognizable, bringing another area of creation within the reach of our consciousness. The impact of the surpassing glory, the wonder and the joy of this new experience is the cause of ecstasy. It is, as it were, that a powerful, long-range telescope has been added to our normally weak mental vision, bringing into sight a hitherto hidden region of creation which is the very antithesis of the world in which we find ourselves now.

Here we live, surrounded by implacable, dead forces of nature; there all is life. Here are death and sorrow; there Life Eternal and immeasurable joy. Here the spirit lives cramped in flesh, inextricably chained to the earth, bewildered by the mystery of its being and tormented by doubt; there is unrestricted freedom, the universe assumes a smiling aspect, the doubt changes into certainty and the sense of bewilderment into ever-increasing wonder at the stupendous Reality, unthinkable and inexpressible, which now absorbs all the attention of the illuminated mind. With this transformation in consciousness man now lands into another area of the universe, where he begins to gain intelligent awareness of the world of Life, as with the dawn of intellect he started to gain an intelligent awareness of the world of matter. This intellectual awareness, though still very, very imperfect, betokens a tremendous advance over all other forms of life on the earth. In the same way the attainment of illuminated consciousness betokens an advance beyond the province covered by the intellect. It is the instinctive recognition of this fact that surrounds the great religious teachers of mankind with a halo of glory that seldom fell to the share of other human beings.

Those who believe that the arousal of Kundalini signifies the activation of an occult or magical force, dormant in the body, which they can manipulate in various ways to gain higher consciousness or miraculous powers, merely exhibit their ignorance and perpetuate their own bondage to superstition. The awakening of Kundalini implies the renewed activity of the same Life-force to refashion the brain to a higher dimension of awareness, which fashions it in the womb and keeps it alive and sane every moment of our life. We know very well that it is not possible for one to interfere, with impunity, with the operation of the mysterious force that keeps our heart beating, our stomach working, our intestines moving, and which is behind the extremely complex activity of the brain. This is the force Kundalini controls and commands.

The yogis who, after years and years of hard and highly dangerous practices, succeed in gaining partial control over their autonomous nervous system, and exhibit their prowess by various feats, such as arrest of the flow of blood, or underground burial for days and even weeks, do so at great risk and often cause irreparable damage to themselves in the process. In the self-induced trance states such yogis often lose consciousness and, even otherwise, are never able to perform those feats of abstract thought and artistic skill which have been the well-spring of all the original creations and achievements of man. There can be nothing more inane than to waste many precious years of one's life in acquiring the ability to cause abnormal conditions of the body for mere spectacular effect, at the cost of the richest treasures of the mind.

The mysterious force of life which is behind all cellular organization can never be apprehended or observed in the same way as a material object. The normal brain equipment is totally dead to this extraordinary radiation. Some gifted individuals glimpse it now and then and so become channels for its manifestation in the form of supernormal sensory perception or psychic gifts. But they, too, have no clue to its mystery.

We have not been able so far to assign a name to this elusive force, what to say of determining its nature or even distantly understanding how it works. It is so remote from all our concepts that, rather than accept the existence of such an unimaginably subtle and complex entity, the world of science has been trying, for the last more than a century now, to formulate mechanical and behavioral theories to account for the phenomenon of life, but all in vain.

The author of Panchastavi has tried to express this incomprehensible aspect of the Cosmic Life-Energy in several verses. In one (V.2), he says: — "(O Goddess) who art beyond the reach of Speech and Logic, able by Thy own essence to awaken (Thy devotees) to the (inner) kingdom of Supreme Bliss (Shiva-Consciousness), shining all over with the lustre of the blue lotus, worthy of adoration even by the Supreme Deity, Shiva, bent with the weight of Thy large, heavy breasts, we make obeisance to Thy entrancing splendor which is beyond the grasp of mind and beyond the power of language to describe." In the light of this honest avowal and knowing well what colossal difficulties are involved in a biological transformation of the brain, down to its deepest layers, what can be said of the claims of those who declare that they are "Masters of Kundalini" and can compass its arousal merely with a touch, a gesture or a look?

Those who forget that they are but drops in the ocean of the Cosmic Life-Energy, the Creatrix of all living beings, themselves stand in need of Grace to purge their minds of the ego that distorts their vision so that they have too high a picture of their own selves. It is never the teacher or the guru but the Divine Power in both of them that leads to the arousal of the Power and liberation of the Soul. This is what our author means (IV.11): — "O Thou Benefactress, (even) for those seekers after salvation, whose actions are balanced and who take shelter in the favor of a guru, it is Thou, O Goddess, who, in a moment, breakest asunder the fetters (of karma) that bind them, and initiates them into the secret teaching of the Shaiva Scriptures."

A highly important office of Yoga and mystical ecstasy is to humble the otherwise inescapable pride of the intellect.

As the only intelligent surveyor of a seemingly barren universe, man is prone to have too high an opinion of himself. In actual fact humanity, at this stage, is like a castaway child trying, without knowing it, to prepare itself for a superhuman role in the aeons to come. But the moderner believes that he has almost attained the zenith of his rise. Experience of *samadhi* or the unitive state in the ruling minds is what is needed to instill feelings of awe and veneration of the unthinkable Reality that unfolds itself in the depths of consciousness. This experience provides the only avenue open to the leading intellects to gain a better insight into the stupendous mystery of creation and also into the soundness of their own thought and deed — a necessary measure for the safety of the race in the atomic age.

A knowledge of the mechanism of Kundalini is thus necessary to change the direction of the human mind. It must know its possibilities and limitations both. The present trends in empirical science make it oblivious to the Cosmic Intelligence ruling every atom and molecule of matter. The very concept of such an All-knowing and All-pervading Consciousness is unacceptable and incomprehensible to it. If accepted it reduces the whole of humanity and all its achievements to a subordinate position and leaves no place for the self-adulation and self-conceit of man.

It is towards the realization of this staggering truth that evolutionary processes are at work in the human frame. Every human being is born to realize that he is a drop of an unbounded Ocean of All-embracing and All-knowing Intelligence. It is only then that his lust for power and possession can cease and peace reign on the earth. He is born to know himself to become aware of the Celestial Glory that has dressed itself in matter to inhabit the earth. There is no escape from the path of evolution aligned for him and the stern laws that rule his life. His only way to peace and happiness lies in cooperating with the regenerative forces that work to draw him upward to his godly stature or pay the forfeit for his revolt in inner and outer disharmony, degeneration and decay. This makes knowledge of Kundalini the most imperative need of our time.

The real aim of Yoga is not unoften incorrectly depicted or understood. The exaggerated love for self tends to paint an entirely opposite picture of the harvest which the practice of the discipline is likely to yield for the aspirant. He imagines all kinds of benefits occurring to himself — peace of mind, transcendence, happiness, miraculous powers, union with the Divine, and the rest. He seldom imagines that the moment the objective of Yoga is achieved, he will cease to be what he is or thinks himself to be. Utterly humbled and subjugated he will then find that he is but a shadow or merely a thin film of ego falsely believing himself to be the doer of deeds and the thinker of thoughts. In fact, all that transpires in the universe, to the slightest movement in the atom, he will see coming from an almighty, unbelievable Intelligence which, in fact, is he, and what he thinks himself to be is but a thin coat of color on That.

This is what the Bhagavad Gita inculcates here (18.61): — "The Lord, O Arjuna, resides in the heart of all beings and makes them revolve on the automaton of the body by His illusive Power (*maya*)." The lifting of this illusive veil is Yoga. Consciousness now comes into its own as the omnipotent Lord of All. The bewildering diversity created by the senses and the mind is dissolved and a new, marvelous picture of the cosmos swims into view. This is the *moksha* of the Indian savants of which the real significance is seldom grasped. It is in this sense that Shakti is addressed as the "Instrument of Liberation" in Panchastavi.

Shiva and Shakti

THE VEIL OF MAYA

Shiva is the same as Brahman of the Upanishads, the primordial Cause behind the Creation. Shakti is His Power to create the universe. In the unmanifested form, i.e. before the universe comes into existence, Shiva and Shakti are one in the unmanifested Sada-Shiva. Bhagavad Gita calls it the unmanifested. "From the Unmanifested," it says (8.18), "all the manifested stream forth at the coming of the day; at the coming of night they dissolve even in That, called the Unmanifested." It is creation that causes the apparent duality. It presents Shiva as the subjective consciousness and Shakti as the objective universe of name and form which is mirrored by the former. The dualism of mind and matter is expressed in Bhagavad Gita (13.20) in these words: - "Know thou that Matter and Spirit are both without beginning, and know thou also that modification and qualities are all Matter born." The Prakriti of Gita is practically the same as the Shakti of the Tantras.

According to Shaiva philosophy, as also according to Vedanta, the two are one. In the former the duality is caused by the Shakti or Creative Energy of the First Cause and, in the latter, by an illusory veil of ignorance known as *maya* which makes the Atman forget its own Divine nature and perceive itself in countless forms as a puny actor in the colossal drama of creation. "Just as power and the possessor of power remain always unseparated, in the same way by virtue of this law the Supreme Lord and His Supreme Energy are both one," says Vijnana Bhairava (18), and adds (19): — "The burning power of fire cannot be thought of as being separate from the fire itself. Only when this insight is gained, that marks the beginning of initiation (true knowledge)." The apparent disparity between the two systems about the nature of Prakriti (matter and its formations) arises primarily on account of two different versions of the same experience. Why this is so will be made clear at another place while discussing *samadhi*.

The point that arises here is why, in Vedanta, the place of precedence is allotted to Brahman and in the Shakta to the Creative Energy or Shakti. According to Vedanta, Brahman is attributeless and *maya* is an inexplicable factor which veils this attributeless Cause of Creation. The result of this superimposition is that the individual soul (Atman) which is Brahman itself, perceives a duality, i.e. itself as the embodied observer, and the colossal world in which it finds itself as the object observed, both separate and distinct from each other.

In actual fact there is no duality. What the Atman perceives is its own projection veiled by *maya*, which makes it appear as the Universe, in the same way as a rope is mistaken for a snake, or mother of pearl for a piece of silver. Thus, even according to Vedanta, the universe is not a myth nor a mere illusion without any substantial base, as has been mistakenly represented by some writers. It is the product of a mistaken perception of one thing for the other. Thus, while all the Universe is Brahman, eternal and undifferentiated, the human mind perceives it as a Multiplicity existing in time and space. This error in perception, it is said, is caused by *avidya*, i.e. lack of real Knowledge or nescience.

There is a world of difference between holding that the world is false or unreal, like the figment of a dream, or that it is the wrong perception of an underlying reality. The latter version, in the context of our present-day knowledge, makes the Vedantic interpretation very significant. It means that the cosmos which we perceive through our senses represents a completely altered picture of a below-the-surface substance which, though actually one, is seen fragmented into an infinite variety of forms in the image. This, in turn, implies that it is not an external agency but the very constitution of our sensory equipment that gives this incomputably multiple shape to one homogeneous stuff which forms the substratum of the Universe. This plainly signifies that the Operation Theatre of the Vedantic *maya* is not located in the cosmos which we perceive, but in the very instrument of perception, that is our brain.

According to the Shakta doctrines, Shakti is both attributeless, without name and form in Her intrinsic form, and also full of attributes, names and forms, when manifested as the universe. At the same time, being the inseparable half of Shiva, She is, in that sense, the created universe and the primordial cause, i.e. Brahman of the Vedanta, in one. The Shakta and, in fact, the Shaiva viewpoint, too, ascribes the phenomenon of creation to One infinite Being beyond the reach of thought, possessed of infinite Energy which transforms itself into the Universe. The Supreme Being, i.e. Shiva Himself, suffers no change in all these gigantic manifestations of activity, like the Brahman of the Upanishads, and continues unaltered through the endless cycles of creation followed, in course of time, by dissolution. This is made clear by Krishna, when displaying His own Universal Form to Arjuna. "But what is the knowledge of all these details to Thee, O Arjuna? Having pervaded this whole Universe with a fragment of myself, I remain." (Bhagavad Gita 10.42).

Every Jiva (embodied soul) is essentially Shiva in His Majesty, only veiled for the time being by the illusive power of His own Shakti or Creative Energy. His release from the individual Consciousness of a Jiva and awareness of Himself as the all-pervading Shiva is also brought about by the same Energy under the sobriquet of Kundalini. With the streaming of Energy into the *sahasrara* (cerebral cortex), a revolution occurs in the strictly limited consciousness of the individual, resulting in the opening of a new channel of perception — the Third Eye — and the apperception of a new, indescribable world of Being which is a concentrated ocean of Existence, Consciousness, Bliss and Beauty personified.

Great importance is attached to the body in the Shakti Shastra. It is the 'Temple of the Divine' and the 'Gateway to Heaven'. It is the *Kshudra-Brahmanda* or 'microcosm' with the same polarization as we see in the universe, the abode of Shiva and Shakti both. The very concept of 'Kaya-Sadhana' or discipline of the body, which forms the central pivot of Hatha-Yoga practices, clearly implies the involvement of the vital organs, nervous system and the brain in the transformation which leads to a new vision of the world or, in other words, to Shiva-Consciousness.

One of the reasons for diversity in the metaphysical concepts about the Absolute and the nature of the manifested universe, which the human soul is always hungry to know, lies in our ignorance about the biological factors responsible for mystical ecstasy. This extraordinary state of consciousness has provided from immemorial times the only avenue for a peep behind the smoke-screen of visible nature. In all ontological speculation the only instrument available to man is the intellect. But this position can change if it is demonstrated that mystical experience or *samadhi* denotes the entry into another dimension of consciousness in which intellect is inoperative and the objective world dissolves into an ocean of being. This shows that the cosmological concepts in the various systems of philosophy as also of science about the nature or the origin of the universe are mere assumptions liable to variation with a change in the pattern of cognitive perception.

According to the worshipers of Shakti, the Atman or conscious principle, clothed in flesh, has no way open to look beyond the world of name and form, presented by its senses and the mind. It is only Shakti, existing in the microcosm of the body at the base of the spine, which can contrive its release by rising up through the spinal cord into *Brahma-randhra* in the brain. When arrived there She unites in a flood of inexpressible rapture with the microcosmic Shiva — the individual conscious principle, and endows it with the supersensory power of cognition by which the transcendental world of being can be perceived.

How Karma Works

In this new dimension of consciousness the ponderous world is relegated to the position of a mirage-like image in the oceanic being of the observer. For the Vedantan, discriminative knowledge of the identity of the Atman and Brahman is enough to tear asunder the veil of *maya* and to realize one's unity with the Supreme Spirit. This discriminative knowledge is not possible without the conditioning of the brain. The transformation of a kind in which the sensory images are proved to be false, in order to be an integral part of the mind and not a delusion, must have its foundation at the neuronic level. In fact, the rarity of the mystical bloom, like the rarity of genius, is a clear indication of the fact that genetic factors are involved. The evolutionary ascent must be accomplished before one can bloom into a *jnani*.

The pre-condition for the attainment of *jnana* is said to be cessation of *samskaras* (causative seeds of previous karma) brought about by a life of striving, dedication and surrender to the Divine will. The doctrine of karma is common to all systems of Yoga and all forms of religious discipline in India. Viewed in the light of modern knowledge, the transmission of the seeds of karma from one life of an individual to another, besides the other spheres of influence, implies the genetic factor also. The very fact that the cessation or ripening of the seeds of karma, done in previous births, is held to be an essential condition for success in the Yogic, Vedantic or Shakta disciplines is a clear testimony to the fact that the biological inheritance and environment of the seeker is a decisive factor in the attainment of the *jnana* state.

A person condemned to blindness, as the harvest of his previous karma, is naturally born blind, another condemned to deafness is born deaf, yet another condemned to a certain kind of ineptitude is born with that particular lack in his mental or physical equipment. Still another, entitled to become a ruler or to pass a life of affluence, is either born in a royal household or a rich family or gifted with mental attributes which raise him to such a position. "If *sattva* verily prevaileth when the embodied goeth to dissolution," says the Bhagavad Gita (14.14), "then he goeth forth to the spotless worlds of the great sages." And further, "Having gone to dissolution in *rajas*, he is born among those attached to action. If dissolved in *tamas* he is born in the wombs of the senseless." (14.15)

The recognition of the fact that the family in which and the mental or physical attributes with which one is born are determined by his previous karma is not only peculiar to Gita but is generally accepted by all the canonical texts of India. Even where there is a difference of opinion about the nature of the Ultimate Reality or the existence of a Divine Creator or even where the authority of the Vedas is not accepted, as for instance in Buddhism, the causative function of karma is readily admitted. It is held to be the determinant of the future birth, involving the psychosomatic endowments and the environment of a human being. That certain biological factors are necessary for success in spiritual striving is clearly admitted in the Bhagavad Gita while discussing the fate of one who falls from the path of Yoga during life. "Or he may even be born into a family of wise yogis, but such a birth as that is most difficult to obtain in this world," says Krishna to Arjuna. "There he receiveth *characteristics belonging to his former body* and with these he again laboreth for perfection, O joy of the Kurus." (6.32-43)

The inference is clear: the very concept of karma carries with it the implication that the karmic seeds in some subtle form survive the death of the tabernacle to determine the future bodily equipment and the external surroundings of the Jiva (embodied soul). There must be, therefore, something in the subtler layers of our organism, beyond the probe of the intellect, in which the seeds of karma take root, grow and bear fruit time after time. There must be something in the structure of the spiritual world on which the thoughts and deeds of mortals leave an indelible mark.

In the context of our present-day knowledge about the human body, what can this ancient belief in reincarnation, based on the fruit of karma, signify? An individual dissolved in *tamas*, i.e., in a state of delusion, holding blindly to the passions and desires of flesh, has to take birth in the wombs of the senseless or, in other words, has to come poorly equipped into the world, according to Gita. We know it well that the heredity and the milieu in which a person is born play a decisive part in regulating his life and career after birth. In this way he reaps the harvest of karma earned in previous incarnations. The moment heredity is involved it ipso-facto implies the involvement of genes and from the genes the whole psychosomatic organism of man, that is, his mind and body both.

The seeds of evil karma that condemn a human being to a life of delusion, suffering and sorrow must, therefore, be present in his genes, which exist in the cells of his brain and in every cell and fibre of his being. Similarly, the merit earned by means of righteous actions that entitles him to liberation, or to a position of power or affluence must also, in the same way, be present in his biological equipment and the environment to enable him to win the reward earned.

When this is admitted — and there appears no other alternative except to admit it — it shall also have to be conceded that those, who ever won to illumination or will be able to win it in future, must be constituted that way with a favorable inner and outer environment. This means, in other words, that they must have a predisposition, both mental and physiological, to reach an enlightened state of consciousness spontaneously or with efforts directed to that end.

But how does karma create favorable or unfavorable circumstances or contrive to build the congenital factors that are necessary for illumination? There is no answer to this riddle either in the ancient spiritual lore of mankind or in the present-day manuals of science. We do not know what determines the mental excellence of a top-rank intellectual or the versatility of a genius and what the clouded thinking of an idiot or the perverted reasoning of a born criminal or cheat. There must be something in the brain of a Vyasa, Shankaracharya, Confucius, Avicena, Shakespeare, Saint Teresa or Paramahamsa Ramakrishna that led them either to the pinnacle of human thought or the zenith of spiritual glory.

There must be something in the brains of all talented men and women in every sphere of thought and skill which is responsible for their outstanding performance, lifting them so high above the average human being that they seem to belong to a class apart. There must be some mystery behind all the revealed scriptures of the earth which held millions upon millions under their sway for thousands of years, and created such revolutions in thought among the multitudes as could never be accomplished by the most powerful kings and emperors throughout the past. At the same time there must be some peculiarity in the brains of genocides, murderers and sadists who take a diabolic pleasure in killing or in causing pain. There must have been some fault in the brain and psychic makeup of all the abominable mass murderers in history. It is easy to say that they were morbid or perverted, megalomaniacs or paranoids, but assigning a name does not explain the biological reasons behind the malady.

A clue to the solution to this profound mystery, which is of the highest importance for humanity, is provided by Panchastavi and other time-honored ancient treatises dealing with the Serpent Power. They contain precious hints which can prove of great value in the investigation directed to explore the ramifications of this wonderful fountain of psychic energy in human beings. Judged from this point of view, this little book, containing no more than 146 verses, couched in a metaphorical vein, crowded with archaic and mythical concepts and notions is yet a valuable guide to a science, still in the making, concerned with the baffling mystery of consciousness. The unknown author of this work unfolds in figurative language the germs of what time will prove to be the greatest discovery ever made by mankind. This discovery, when pursued further with the methods known to science, will not only throw light on the still obscure problems of mind, but also start a chain of revolutionary thinking till the whole area of human life becomes transformed in consonance with the still hidden laws ruling the spiritual destiny of the human race.

NORMAL AND PARANORMAL PERCEPTION

This little digression to show the close connection between the doctrine of karma and the biological endowment of man has been made to throw light on the position that there is another world of being, always round and above us, of which we remain in the dark through all the period of our earthly existence. Somewhere at the subatomic level of our bodies there is a mysterious interconnection between that world and our mortal coils which is always beyond the range of our perception. We have no idea what forces act and what laws operate in these subliminal depths and how they influence our thought and act so that we voluntarily reap the fruit of what we have sown. Our own concepts of law and justice, sin and punishment, we owe to the same boundless Reservoir of thought from which all our notions and ideas come. Therefore, how can we suppose that the Fountainhead from which we draw our being and our inspiration would be itself devoid of that law and order which we borrow from it? There must be a system of absolute justice ruling the forces of life as there are stern laws ruling the forces of matter in the universe.

A fish in water can never imagine the charming and highly extended panorama open to the eye of a bird. In the same way, a normal mind can never frame a picture of the marvelous vista open to the inner eye of a yogi, whose brain is attuned to the finer vibrations of life. There are worlds within worlds and wheels within wheels in creation which are entirely impervious to our senses. Intellectually we have outgrown the stage when it could be said that a Recording Angel or some other supernatural entity is always busy in maintaining an indelible inventory of our actions good or bad. The mythical figure of Yama or a divine functionary is no longer necessary to explain how the actions of human beings are recorded and screened to meet the ends of celestial law and justice. The subtle mechanisms of life, in operation in the psychosomatic structure of every individual, can perform the task more efficiently and thoroughly than any angel or supernal being could do. The same devices that rule heredity operate the law of Karma also. All this happens in a world completely shut out from our view. Those who believe in karma or supernal justice must also believe in worlds beyond our ken.

We have absolutely no control over nor even awareness of the subtle organic forces working in our body. Science has not so far been able to locate or even coin names for them. It is only now that study of the so-called bioenergy or bioplasma has been undertaken at some places. But the extreme subtlety and the elusive nature of the stuff makes the task difficult in the extreme. Therefore, in dealing with Kundalini, we deal with a fringe subject which is yet beyond the province of modern science. The fact that the Society for Psychical Research and, more recently, Parapsychology have accumulated volumes of evidence to prove that psi phenomena are a reality does not mean that they have gleaned the least knowledge about the force at the back. Similarly, the piles of volumes on biological sciences do not make us the least wiser about the mysterious cause behind the phenomena of life.

"We do not apprehend man as a whole," says Alexis Carrell, "Each one of us is made up of a procession of phantoms, in the midst of which strides an unknowable reality." [4] No one can deny that an impenetrable wall divides the surface consciousness of man from the inscrutable subliminal forces which maintain the flame of life in his body. We do not even know how we live. This is what Goethe means when he says: - "But in general man has to grope his way. He knows not whence he came nor whither he goes. He knows little of the world and himself least of all." [7]

The experiments of Uri Geller, though open to doubt so far as psychokinesis is concerned, provide very strong evidence for telepathy. [8] The reason why scientific opinion is still divided about paranormal phenomena is because they are rare, erratic and unpredictable. But the volume of evidence gathered so far in our time and the persistent appearance of the faculty in some individuals, through the whole course of history, leave no room for doubt about their occurrence. To reject them is to provide evidence not of the open-minded attitude of scientific inquiry but of narrow prejudice of a stubborn kind. The slowly mounting weight of unquestionable evidence is building up a pressure on the recalcitrant scientific mind that cannot now be resisted for long. Large cracks in the structure are already visible to the discerning eye.

Universal acceptance of paranormal phenomena poses a problem for modern science for which there is no solution except a radical change in its current concepts about mind and the universe as a whole. This would involve a thorough recasting of the existing world of modern thought to its very foundations. The very laws and forces on which the whole massive structure of science is built will then come under fire. No study of the human brain would then be considered complete unless, in addition to intelligence and talent, it included extrasensory perception also. It is only then that a complete picture of the complex human personality will begin to emerge.

Genius is rare. So are outstanding paranormal gifts. The really good mediums are as scarce as really great poets, artists or thinkers. But while the exceptionally intelligent brain has been subjected to minute examination, whenever possible during the past many decades to locate the cause behind them, psychic gifts have never been taken seriously enough to elicit the same attention. This shows how erratically the human mind works even in this age of unfettered freedom of enquiry and research.

"If paranormal cognition and paranormal causation are facts," says Professor Broad in an article, "then it is quite likely that they are not confined to those very rare occasions on which they either manifest themselves sporadically in a spectacular way, or to those very special conditions in which their presence can be experimentally established. They may well be continually operating in the background of our normal lives." This means, in other words, that paranormal cognition and causation might be a below-the-surface part of our mental endowment. It is not necessary to adduce special empirical proof for the supposition. Emergence of paranormal faculties in hypnotic trance, in dreams and semi-awake conditions, in individuals who do not evince them in the waking state, is enough to establish the fact. But if paranormal cognition is a property of the human mind, there must be provision for it in the brain also.

But what is the mystery behind these strange occurrences which do not fit in with our everyday image of the universe and, if accepted as valid, force us to revise the picture presented by our senses? In trying to explain the paradoxical nature of clairvoyant perception, Sir Cyril Burt writes:

> "Our sense organs and our brain operate as an intricate kind of filter which limits and directs the mind's clairvoyant powers, so that under normal conditions attention is concentrated on just those objects or situations that are of biological importance for the survival of the organism and its species. . . . As a rule, it would seem that the mind rejects ideas coming from another mind as the body rejects grafts coming from another body."[9]

With slight modifications the same idea is expressed by several other scholars, including William James and Henri Bergson. In the view of Aldous Huxley the brain acts as a reducing valve in respect of the paranormal to eliminate the flood of impressions that can, by causing confusion, otherwise seriously endanger survival. It is rather strange that even those courageous savants who, either out of their own experiences or on the strength of the evidence gathered, believe in the reality of psychic phenomena should still hold to the duality of the normal and paranormal, as if they are, in actual fact, two different and distinct entities. A more rational assessment would be to treat mystical experiences, oceanic feelings and paranormal gifts as the expressions of a dormant faculty still in the process of emergence, provided by nature to supplement the knowledge gathered through the already existing sensory channels and the intellect.

"One way of stating the situation," says Gardner Murphy, "is that paranormal processes do not represent a part of the time-space-event system which physical science describes. As we have suggested above there is a certain timeless, spaceless, or we might say transtemporal and transpatial character at the very heart of the paranormal. This is, indeed, one of the major reasons why the phenomena do not belong to and are rejected by official science."[10] This brings us to the very core of the problem that engaged the attention of the Indian savants for centuries, culminating in those systems of psychosomatic discipline which are grouped under the general name of Yoga. The aim of these disciplines is to force into operation a still developing supersensory channel of cognition in the human brain to gain entry to the transtemporal and transpatial plane, imperceptible to the normal mind.

Some of the most inspiring passages in the Bhagavad Gita relate to the vision of the Cosmic Form shown by Krishna to Arjuna as the Lord of the Universe. This unmistakably refers to the breathtaking experience of Super-Consciousness encountered in *samadhi*. "Here, today, behind the whole Universe, movable and immovable," says Krishna (2.7-8), "standing in one in my body, O Gudakesha (Arjuna), with aught else thou desirest to see . . . . But verily thou art not able to behold me with these thine eyes; the divine eyes I give unto thee. Behold My Sovereign Yoga." This 'divine eye' refers to the extraordinary channel of perception which is the ultimate target of every form of Yoga and every spiritual discipline. This presupposes evolution of the brain and, consequent on that, transformation of human consciousness towards a new dimension in which paranormal cognition and a new vision of the Universe, as experienced in mystical ecstasy, become possible. The marvelous world to which mind and consciousness belong now stands revealed to the initiate.

"Men who have no riches, who live on recognized food, who have perceived the 'Void' and 'Unconditional Freedom' (nirvana), their path is difficult to understand, like that of birds in the air," says Buddha in *Dhammapada* (VII.3), while describing the Arhat. The path of the enlightened is difficult to understand because they are differently constituted, because their cognition of the objective world has undergone a change, because, in addition to the stimuli coming from the senses, there pours into the mind a wealth of impressions from other layers of creation of such indescribable glory and beatitude that all the delights of earth appear trivial in comparison.

Paranormal gifts which, at the moment, form a subject of extensive research all over the world, are nothing but sporadic elusive symptoms of a new development that is occurring in the human brain. They appear inexplicable, weird and erratic because our vision is clouded and because our mind has not yet attained the state of knowledge where these transphysical forces can be recognized and cataloged. A modern jetliner with a gaily attired crowd of passengers, passing every now and then over a primitive habitation of the neolithic age, would be regarded with extreme superstitious awe as a visitation from another world. We fail to ascribe our incapacity to explain psychic phenomena to the fault of the intellect because, like the primitives, we have no knowledge that there are other beings and other forces in creation that can bring to pass what seem impossibilities to us.

In spite of all the marvels of modern technology to its credit, the rationalist view of the cosmos is the very antithesis of the actual position. It is not matter but consciousness which is the ultimate reality of the Universe. This is the basic tenet of the Vedanta and Shaiva philosophies. This is also the basic datum of observation in *samadhi*. The world we see is the creation of the senses and the mind. We can never succeed in detecting this illusion unless the instrument of perception, i.e. consciousness, undergoes a change. This is what Yoga is designed to achieve. Change in consciousness necessarily implies a change in the basic structure of the brain. This cannot be achieved by any means whatsoever save by the arousal and metabolic activity of Kundalini.

Paranormal events are not, in reality, beyond the range of the normal nor do they subvert the known laws of physics, but they serve simply as a reminder of the untenable nature of our own assumptions. Psychic powers have always been considered to be a singular possession of the saint, the seer and the prophet. But the real distinguishing feature of all these classes of holy people has been ecstasy, often with inspired oracular utterance and prophesy.

It is ironic that in this age of vastly extended knowledge this one singular characteristic of illumination, always recognized throughout the past, is almost completely lost sight of in the study of mystical or psychic phenomena. This failure to grasp a most noteworthy characteristic of higher consciousness is, in turn, sadly reflected in the failure of the crowds of seekers to distinguish the true adept from the false. This has led to the anomalous position that the modern, well-informed aspirants entirely omit to take notice of the one outstanding attribute of a spiritual teacher that was considered to be an invariable feature of enlightenment even in the dark ages, namely an inspired personality.

"This overcoming of all the usual barriers between the individual and the Absolute," says William James, "is the great mystic achievement. In mystic states we both become one with the Absolute and we become aware of our oneness. This is the everlasting and triumphant mystical tradition hardly altered by differences of clime or creed. In Hinduism, in Neoplatonism, in Sufism, in Christian mysticism, in Whitmanism, we find the same recurring note, so that there is about mystical utterances an eternal unanimity which ought to make a critic stop and think, and which brings it about that the mystical classics have, as has been said, neither birthday nor native land. Perpetually telling of the unity of man with god, their speech antidates languages and they do not grow old."

"The great field for this sense of being the instrument of a higher power," adds James at another place, "is, of course, 'inspiration'. It is easy to discriminate between the religious leaders who have been habitually subject to

inspiration and those who have not. In the teachings of
the Buddha, of Jesus, of Saint Paul (apart from his gift
of tongues), of Saint Augustine, of Huss, of Luther, of
Wesley, automatic or semi-automatic composition appears
to have been only occasional. In the Hebrew prophets,
on the contrary, in Mohammed, in some of the
Alexandrians, in many minor Catholic saints, in Fox, in
Joseph Smith, something like it appears to have been
frequent, sometimes habitual."[11]

The account of William James makes no mention of cases
in India in which the faculty of inspired utterance developed
with the practice of Yoga and the development of Kundalini,
as in the cases of Kabir, Guru Nanak, Ramakrishna, and
others. The authors of Panchastavi and Saundarya Lahari
plainly ascribe the bloom of their own poetic talent to the
ministrations of the Divine Power. In fact, the constant
allusion to 'speech' and 'sound' and 'the letters of the
alphabet' in the books on Shri Vidya clearly points to the
conclusion that inspired expression and oracular utterance
were prized as the highest boon possible with the disciplines
aimed to arouse the Serpent Power.

The term 'automatic' coined by modern psychology to
denote the class of utterance or writing which comes without
conscious effort is inapt even in respect of the ordinary cases
of this type, and highly misleading when applied to the
inspired utterances of great prophets and seers. It is generally
held that all expressions of this kind come from the
'unconscious'. But what in reality is the 'unconscious' or
'subconscious'? Is it a foreign entity or the submerged part
of our own personality which, because of a certain lack of
adjustment in the mechanism of the brain, remains
inaccessible to the conscious effort of the average individual.
If we predicate the existence of a 'Cosmic Mind', then
'Higher Consciousness' clearly means an 'enhanced
awareness' brought about by a greater liaison between the
brain and the 'Cosmic Reservoir'.

There is no difference of opinion among the various schools of psychologists about the enormous potential present in the 'unconscious'. It is held that our normal waking consciousness represents only the visible peak of a huge mountain submerged under the waters of an ocean. But the submerged part, too, must have a place in the activity of the brain. Otherwise it can never become a causative factor in dreams, in automatism, in inspiration, in hypnosis, in clairvoyance, in multiple personality, in behavioral complexes and in insanity. We do not know the nature of the relationship between the brain and the mind as here we deal with subtle entities and mechanisms beyond the frontiers reached by science. But there can be no doubt that these entities and mechanisms do exist and are operative in us for it is to them that we owe our individuality and our life. The only channel provided by nature to reach this otherwise forbidden province is Kundalini.

THE WONDER OF HIGHER CONSCIOUSNESS

What Panchastavi implies by the term 'Shakti' is the Intelligent Power behind the Supra-rational world of life and consciousness. Kundalini is the key to open the door to this amazing world. Whatever a mortal is in his thoughts, feelings, will, imagination, talents, merits or faults, all come from this world. Just as all the lights of every conceivable design in a city receive their power from one and the same source, so the light of awareness in every living creature comes from this world of Cosmic Life-Energy or Shakti.

She is the World-Charmer, invisible Herself, yet enveloping the embodied soul in a veil of illusion. She is the seductive female drawing man to the bed of enjoyment and at the same time, the compassionate Mother who, at the opportune time, breaks asunder the fetters that bind him to the prisonhouse of the body and the earth, leading him to the glorious summit of self-realization. She is, in short, the arbiter of human destiny. It is through Her beguiling powers that mortals are entangled in the web of illusion and through Her liberative office that they are released from it.

"How strange it is, O Mother," says Panchastavi (IV.17), "that this ocean of illusion (i.e. this creation born of *maya*) confusingly crowded with countless cosmic hosts like bubbles (on its surface), filled with waves of (countless) diverse kinds of affliction, with the submarine fire, generated by constant meditation on Thee, is destroyed in an instant (i.e. is dissolved into consciousness)." The concept of 'maya' or the illusive power of 'Shakti' is extremely hard for the intellect to accept, especially one engaged in the empirical study of organic life. But the concept is, at least, as old as the Vedas and has been tested and retested in the crucible of yogic experience for thousands of years.

It is now impossible to form an idea of the colossal effort that has gone into the formation of this concept and its present position as an almost universal belief among the Hindu population of India. The germs of the theory exist in the Vedas, but the first clear expression of it is contained in the Upanishads. How far back the concept was evolved and to what distance it must have traveled, in the proto-historic period, is illustrated by an event in the life of Janaka, a philosopher-king par excellence, and one of the key figures among the hierarchy of enlightened sages mentioned in the Upanishads.

According to Dr. S.B. Roy, a noted Indologist, the renowned queen Theyi of the 18th dynasty of Egypt (1416-1370 B.C.), was not only acquainted with, but also subscribed to the philosophy of Janaka. It was under her influence that her son, the great Akhenaton, modeled his own life after Janaka, the philosopher-king of India. There still exists today, says Dr. Roy, the remnants of the famous banyan tree under which Janaka convened his philosophic conferences. From Egypt the influence of the philosophy must have traveled to Greece. The basic structure on which the concept of 'maya' or 'maya-Shakti' has been built is provided by the experience of *samadhi.* The world of name and form undergoes a radical transformation in the *turiya* or fourth state of consciousness.

There is a gulf between the normal human consciousness and the *turiya* state which not even the most fertile imagination can fill up. Wonder, unbounded and endless, is a pronounced characteristic of it. "O thou Mine of Wonders," says the author of Panchastavi addressing the Shakti (V.21). "This Wonder, this One, to which in verity no name may be given," is how Plotinus describes the state.[12] It is impossible to describe the overwhelming state of astonishment which fills the soul when, with the inflow of the new psychic currents into the brain, the area of individual consciousness begins to widen until, like an ocean, it spreads everywhere as far as the mind can reach. The surprise and the concomitant sense of unutterable happiness do not end after once they are experienced. But, like an unceasing succession of waves racing across an ocean, come again and again in an endless chain to sweep over the entranced yogi during the whole period of ecstatic contemplation.

It is not hard to imagine the state of mind of one who, in full wakefulness, finds himself lifted up by an invisible force, carried through space at unbelievable speed and dropped suddenly on the leaping waters of Niagara Falls. His amazement at the inexplicable occurrence and his terror, when he lands on the rushing torrent about to plunge into the thundering, seething, fearsome cauldron below, will know no bounds. But inexpressible would be his wonder when he finds that he is able to tread nimbly, light as a feather, on the descending sheet of roaring water and to walk swiftly on the foaming whirlpools at the bottom, as if on a firm surface, impervious to the fury of the boiling mass raging and swirling all around him.

The feeling of stark terror, experienced at first, would yield place to a sense of overpowering awe at the uncanny nature of the whole adventure and the person involved may pinch himself to make sure whether he is dreaming or whether what he is witnessing is really true. But his amazement would grow and grow as he continued to observe his own incredible performance in this supernatural drama, darting here and there, alive and kicking, in the dreadful maelstrom of water, just below the falls, like a dancing ray of light, as if beyond the pale of the laws of earth.

The same would be the state of breathless surprise of one dropped on the perpetual snowy cap of Mount Everest, able to roam and skip merrily from one peak to the other as if an invisible buoyant stuff helped to keep his body afloat and propelled it from one summit to another. When the first shock is over, one who finds himself in such a strange situation, made increasingly aware that what he perceives is real, would sing ecstatically out of sheer exhilaration at the stupendous feat. Or, if of a contemplative bent of mind, he would remain absorbed in the survey of the marvelous vista opened to his eyes on every side. Dancing with joy at this sudden release from the trammels of earth, he might never cease to wonder at this unparalleled stroke of luck, when he finds that he can now move round the earth, at will, and visit his old haunts, unseen by all, impervious to hunger, thirst, sleep and other needs of the body, as if transformed into another being and transferred to another way of life.

We can multiply such examples indefinitely to illustrate the point. The human mind, accustomed from birth to the pigeon-hole of the body, susceptible to its needs and restricted by the limitations of its senses, when suddenly brought face to face with its native state of freedom is so struck by wonder and so thrilled to the core by the new experience that language fails to describe the transport and the emotions felt. The current misconception about Yoga and the distortions to which it is subjected are due to the fact that the stupendous nature of the transformation wrought in the entire being of an initiate by the supreme experience is still not realized clearly by those interested in the phenomenon.

The experience of flying in dreams is common to many people. So is that of falling from a height or leaping down from a summit or the roof of a building onto the ground, or of a sheet of water falling into a void below. Many people wake up suddenly from such a dream, even before the impact of the fall, with rapidly beating hearts and a sense of fear, sometimes mixed with surprise at the extraordinary escape from harm. Since judgement is usually blunted in the dream condition and the intellect confused, the dreaming ego fails to assess correctly the impact of the experience. In real life the same experience can be shattering in the extreme. It would be an incredible and unbelievable performance. From this one instance we can frame a hazy picture of the overwhelming effect on one's mind caused by the bodiless peregrinations of the soul in the state of *samadhi* with all the faculties fully alert, and even more acute than in the normal waking state.

The current misconceptions about the ecstatic state are due to the fact that we are accustomed to treat the normal waking state of the human mind as the standard of measurement to adjudge it. This is wrong, as it can never be possible to arrive at the correct evaluation of an object with a defective measuring yardstick. The normal human awareness is a contracted and contorted form of the transcendental consciousness which is the evolutionary target of the human race. Compared to the bloom that has to occur in it one day, the present state of awareness is like the first grey flush of dawn compared to the brilliant lustre cast by the fully risen morning sun.

Dazzled by the intensity of their own vision, mystics of all ages were never able to make the curious crowds their partners in the secret. They always remained a class apart, able to command their homage, but unable to raise them to their own level. The irony is that the intellectual, well versed in the knowledge of the day and confident of his own vast range of information, is as much at a disadvantage here as an ignorant being. The reason for this is that it is an entirely foreign territory to both.

The glowing narratives of the mystics of all climes about their extraordinary states, the sublime descriptions of Brahman in the Upanishads, the glorious vision of the Universal Being portrayed in the Gita, the panegyrics sung to Kundalini (Shakti) in Panchastavi and Saundarya Lahari and the inspiring prayers and lauds addressed to God, Shiva, Christ, Krishna, Allah, and all other deities in the whole religious literature of mankind are but fervent tributes paid to this crowning state of consciousness — the natural heritage of the future man and woman.

In the true mystical experience a sense of unbounded wonder and profound awe fills the mind for the whole period of its duration. The hairs literally stand on end at the solemn breathtaking nature of the spectacle. The ego, proud of its accomplishments — learning, wisdom, power, possession, wealth or beauty — is humbled to dust, completely overpowered and eclipsed by the indescribably majestic aspect of the vision unfolded before the inner eye. Gone are the ideas of greatness, of command, of riches, of piety, superiority and of all other considerations which self-love and pride beget in us. The soul, now divested of all the appendages imposed by the body, the senses and the mind, brought face to face with its own divine substance, beyond anything encountered before, is transfixed with amazement at the stupendous transformation and plunged into such a state of wonder and rapture that it is beyond the power of pen to describe.

It is the incredible nature of the 'stuff' behind the phenomenon of life that makes it so hard for the realistic to accept its existence. The moment he does so he finds the solid ground which holds the weight of all his world of thought slipping from under his feet. But for any picture of the cosmos to be complete there must be a plausible explanation for religious experience and psychic phenomena also. No system of modern philosophy and no explanation provided by science presents a complete solution to the riddle of life. The Darwinian theory of evolution can be likened to a miller's attempt to explain the whole world of meteorological phenomena in terms of his own windmill. A stupendous ocean of invisible activity is hidden behind every living creature on the earth. It is the vision of this marvelous but invisible other world that makes *samadhi* the most breathtaking experience possible to man. The whole fabric of Panchastavi is vibrant with the stunning effect of this encounter on the author's mind.

Even in terms of the Darwinian hypothesis the drama, enacted by life on earth, is an incredible performance beyond anything our mind can visualize. We fail to notice its sublime character because every effort has been made to minimize this performance to bring it within the orbit of a narrow intellectual formulation. The same intellect which formed the hypothesis is now gathering the data to demolish it. Direct refutation of the theory lies in the very constitution of the human mind. Its capacity to design and plan, to invent and discover, its deep-rooted sense of law and order, its love for reasoning and thought, aesthetics and ideals and its insatiable thirst for knowledge and unappeasable hunger to know itself are so alien to the forces which, according to Darwin, compassed the birth and evolution of life that no further argument to refute it is necessary.

A retrospect of the drama, even on the lines laid down by the evolutionists, presents a picture which, in the light of what we now know about the violently changing states of the earth, makes the academic story unbelievable.

Terrestrial life was born out of the battle of elements as sparks are born out of the friction of stones. It is impossible to imagine, at this distance of billions of years, the stormy condition of the earth's crust when the initial forms of life are said to have first made their appearance in the shallow, slimy waters of seas and lakes. The scalding rays of the sun that shone upon those waters, the tempestuous gales that lashed them to violent motion and the torrential rains that furiously beat upon them are beyond our imagination now. A faint picture of this scene can be evoked by comparing it to a furious desert storm, so hot that it blisters the skin, so violent that it uproots enormous trees and so laden with dust that it buries whole cities under mounds of sand as if they had never existed at all. The struggle for existence is, therefore, inherent in the very nature of life from the time of its first appearance on earth.

The living essence that survived the onslaught of millions of years, withstood the fury of elemental rage, and bore rigors of climate that cannot even be pictured now, must have had a power of endurance in it that no adversity could crush. What this invisible and apparently frail essence, battling heroically with the relentless, warring elements of nature every moment of its existence, has achieved during these thousands of million years is so staggering as to be inconceivable, were not the proof before our eyes on every side. Considered in the context of its history through the stormy past, extending to so vast a span of time that the whole period of the existence of man constitutes but a small fraction of it, there is no event so marvelous in the whole creation as the march of life from the primary cell to man, now devising ways and means, after the conquest of earth, to dominate other distant planets in space.

When one contemplates the earth with all its countless varieties of organic structures on land, in the depths of the ocean and in the air, it seems inconceivable that any unbiased intelligent mind can be hurried into the belief with assiduous indoctrination from young age that this stupendous display could be the result of unplanned and aimless chemical organization of matter, unaware of both its beginning and the end. The crowning glory of this battle for survival that raged on land, in the sea and in the air for millions of years, is man with his still untapped depth of imagination and thought. What, therefore, began as an infinitely minute spark of sentience in the primary forms of life and culminated in the marvelous world of thought in man through a herculean struggle lasting for ages must, therefore, be something so tough, so indomitable, so persistent and so remote from the wildest flights of our thought that we fail to grasp its existence at all. "The nature of the psyche reaches into obscurities far beyond the scope of our understanding," says Jung. "It contains as many riddles as the universe with its galactic systems, before whose majestic configurations only a mind lacking in imagination can fail to admit its own insufficiency. This extreme uncertainty of human comprehension makes the intellectualistic hubbub not only ridiculous, but also deplorably dull."

The invisible, tenuous medium that has been responsible for this wonderful transformation of the rocky, barren, storm-lashed and sun-scorched surface of the earth, through aeonian spans of time, the architect of countless most intelligently fashioned forms, varying in size from the giant dinosaurs to invisible bacteria, cannot be of a capricious or ephemeral nature but must have a hold on matter, a duration in time, boundless wisdom and unlimited potency beyond anything that the puny intellect can conceive of. A mind that has no knowledge about its own nature and is not even able to fathom its own subliminal depths nor understand the intricacies of the body in which it lives is not in a position, because of its inherent limitations, to apprehend the inconceivable proportions of the superintelligent force which runs through every creature, large and small, wherever life is found, from one end of the universe to the other.

The issue with which we are concerned here is whether the inherent tendencies of this Life-Force that has built a marvelous kingdom over the whole surface of the earth, to the deepest depths of the ocean and the highest summits of lofty mountains, can be made to deflect from its course by the willful efforts of man. For example, if man is destined to attain to a far richer bloom of his mind, beyond the wildest dreams of our leading thinkers, by the same process of organic evolution by which he occupies the present preeminent position among all the other forms of earthly life, can any individual or the race as a whole, by their own efforts contrive to retard this process and defeat the aim of nature in the long run? It is a momentous issue on which the future of mankind can depend.

In order to answer this question the first thing to ascertain is whether human beings, individually or collectively, have the capacity to kill completely or alter the direction of their own inherent tendencies. Have they the power to master their innate desires and passions at their own will and choice? We know that save, perhaps, in an extremely limited number of cases this has never been possible so far. Efforts directed to inhibit a natural instinct, we find, recoil adversely on the individual. We also know that, in order to maintain an even flow of the stream of life, there exist polarities not only in the individual but collectively in the race also which correct or neutralize uneven tendencies by mutual reaction.

This conflict of trends and aptitudes among human beings can be likened to the dashing and clashing of countless waves on the surface of an ocean when contrary winds beat upon it from every side. For instance, non-violence has to contend with violence, pacifism with aggression, abstention with indulgence, charity with extortion, poverty with wealth, virtue with vice, ambition with content, cruelty with mercy, austerity with luxury, chastity with licentiousness, and so on. What can be the incredible nature of the omniscient Intelligence whose manipulation of these innumerable things keeps a mighty host of billions of individuals on the highway prescribed for it? The present division of the human world into warring ideological camps provides a tangible proof for this fact. The whole of mankind stands helpless before this ominous rift. Why, with all our rationality, knowledge and wealth of resources, are we not able to heal it? And yet the discord might be aimed to serve a purpose essential for the evolution of the race.

There are dormant forces in the human psyche which not only regulate the behavior of individuals in their daily life and by creating conflicts and pressures sway their course of action, but which also come to the surface in large-scale countrywide revolts and revolutions or global upheavals. It is on this colossal drama of the inner world that the curtain is lifted by Kundalini. We never know that there exists a boundless ocean of thought in which the stellar universes and the countless hosts of living creatures have their being, like bubbles on the surface of a sea, and that it is the vision of this inconceivable Reality which unfolds itself before the blessed in *samadhi*. The experience can be infinitely varied because biological and constitutional factors are involved. But it is towards a perfect unfoldment of this Cosmic Vision that the human brain is modeling itself. The ideas expressed appear to us strange and our author's eulogy on the Goddess seems overdone because we cannot imagine even distantly the breathtaking, stupendous Power to which he alludes.

Mystical Experience and Modern Science

MIND AND BRAIN

*I*n Panchastavi, as in other hymns of praise to the Shakti (Cosmic Energy), the position of standing of the heavenly hierarchy is reversed. Brahma the Creator, Vishnu the Preserver, and Shiva the Destroyer are no longer the supreme autocratic rulers of the universe, but now hold a position subordinate to the primordial Shakti. In some representations of the Goddess they are shown carrying Her throne on their shoulders, like attendants meekly carrying the palanquin of a queen. Her imposing figure is shown sitting on the throne in royal style, while the mighty gods stand humbly to carry out Her commands.

In other representations She is shown dancing on the prostrate form of Shiva, frightful in appearance, with a garland of human skulls round Her neck, Her mouth dripping blood, a severed human head in one of Her hands and an upraised sword in the other, wearing the aspect of a destructive or avenging Fury whose awful might no god can resist. She is Kali, the emblem of Destruction and the personification of Time which swallows everything. This ancient representation of the Cosmic Energy as Kali, interpreted in the language of science, symbolizes the principle of entropy, by which all organized forms of matter tend to disintegrate into lower and still lower levels of organization until, like a giant machine, the whole universe would dissolve into its primal constituents whose nature has not even been determined so far.

As Durga, the Cosmic Energy or Shakti symbolizes the principle of syntropy which is opposed to entropy. Under the influence of this principle matter tends to reach higher and higher levels of organization, order and harmony. The evolution of life on earth and, maybe, even on other planets in the universe is the outcome of this principle of syntropy in matter. Viewed from this angle, Durga is the creative and Kali the destructive aspect of the Cosmic Energy. By the universal law of decay the already existing universe is tending towards dissolution but, amid this all-pervasive process of decay, life has built itself into an organic kingdom of extreme complexity and marvelous organization on the earth. The human brain represents the most finished product of this process. With the awakening of Kundalini this organic masterpiece attains a still higher organization, leading to another dimension of consciousness in which other wonders of creation open to the vision of man.

The doctrine of Shakti is thus of profound cosmic significance. In the microcosmic form the universal principle of entropy works in the organic kingdom also. After the expiry of a prescribed period of time, when a living body has attained a certain state of maturity, the process of decline sets in ending in death. The process is, as a rule, irreversible and death is inevitable for every creature born. But even in this tendency to decay and dissolution, evinced by the human body after maturity, the arousal of Kundalini leads to the renewed activity of Durga to rescue the creature from the fear of extinction and death. The brain is processed until the deathless glory of the soul manifests itself.

The first verse of the second canto of Panchastavi refers to this supreme office of Shakti or Kundalini. Indra is the soul, the chief of the Devatas, i.e. the noble tendencies in the human psyche. Mahishasura is the head of the animal or demoniac propensities who overpowers the gods and with his evil host turns to fight Durga who comes to their rescue. The Cosmic Energy, astride a lion, kills the demons, resulting in the victory of the gods. The appellation, Buffalo, applied to the head of the demons is significant. It is symbolic of the slothful, indolent mind dead to spiritual values and ideals, wallowing in the mire of sensual pleasure, dragging the soul deeper and deeper into the unrelieved darkness of carnal life.

This epic battle between the Devas and Asuras (the gods and the demons) is fought in the body of every human being. It is only through the Grace of Durga (Kundalini) that faults in the *pranic* body can be cured. When freed of evil, man can march towards the ideal of perfection prescribed for him. Every prophet, saint and savior ever born, every reformer and every human being of noble virtue and benevolent disposition who ever contributed to make the earth a better and happier place to live in, owed every bit of the merit possessed to the ministrations of Durga, the benign Cosmic Life-Energy working in every human frame.

Impartial assessment of the monuments left by the ancient Egyptians makes it increasingly clear that they possessed a sure intuitive knowledge of the laws and forces of nature which science is now finding out through laborious observation and experiment. There is no other explanation for the remarkable skill and ingenuity displayed in the construction of the Great Pyramid and other archaeological wonders of the time. A scientific study of Kundalini will lead ultimately to the same conclusion. It will then be found that nineteenth century science gravely blundered in drawing conclusions too hastily about life and the state of knowledge in the ancient world. Scientists of our day, influenced by the skeptical atmosphere still prevailing in many of the universities, find it hard to accept what is becoming increasingly manifest — that life and consciousness cannot be explained in terms of the known chemical and physical properties of matter. Some other still unsuspected form of energy, not conforming to the known laws of physics, has to be postulated to account for the phenomenon of mind.

A wind of change has already started to blow in the province of biology and psychology which augurs a broader outlook on the still unexplained phenomenon of life in the future. Writing under the heading, "A Threat to Darwinism", Stephen Jay Gould says in a recent article:

> "But something even more fundamental is threatened, namely Darwinism itself. The Darwinian theory of evolution relies upon natural selection to preserve favorable variants and eliminate unfavorable ones. With neutralism we have no control by selection since neutral alleles are invisible to natural selection. While neutralists acknowledge that some alleles have selective significance, they claim that only a small proportion of the total variation in natural populations reflects a control by selection. Darwinian selection, metaphorically speaking, is a wind that can only move the superficial skin of a deep ocean of variability." [13]

In the department of psychology an article by Dr. Wilder Penfield sums up the present position about brain and mind in the concluding lines. "Because it seems to me certain," he says, "that it will always be quite impossible to explain the mind on the basis of neuronal action within the brain, and because it seems to me that the mind develops and matures independently through an individual's life, as though it were a continuing element and because a computer (which the brain is) must be programmed and operated by an agency capable of independent understanding, I am forced to choose the proposition that our being is to be explained on the basis of two fundamental elements. This, to my mind, offers the greatest likelihood of leading us to the final understanding towards which so many stalwart scientists strive."[14] The Agency capable of independent understanding which operates the brain, in the words of Penfield, already discovered by the Yoga adepts of India and dealt with in innumerable works, is none other than Prana-Shakti, the Cosmic Life-Energy behind all the phenomena of mind and consciousness. Kundalini is the Key to the Mystery of this almighty Power beyond the scrutiny of the intellect.

Dr. Roger W. Sperry, Professor of Psychobiology, is equally explicit in an article on human values:

> "But this kind of reasoning," he says, referring to the materialistic view that value judgments lie outside science, "no longer holds in terms of mind-brain theory which is more mentalistic and now allows, in principle, a scientific treatment of subjective mental phenomena, including values as causal agents. Also, we now recognize that facts are always interpreted by brain processes, which are already inherently goal-directed, with inbuilt value constraints . . . . Today's modified concept of function allows for mind-matter interaction within the brain. I describe this view as one which places mind in the driver's seat in command over matter. It idealizes ideas and ideals over physio-chemical interactions, and recognizes conscious mental forces as the crowning achievement of evolution."[15]

What Sir Charles Sherrington, the well-known authority on the brain, had opined in 1947, "that our being should consist of two fundamental elements (brain and mind) offers, I suppose, no greater inherent improbability than that it should rest on one only," is now receiving the support of many other eminent scientists. But what is still hard to accept for them is the fact that this second element in the composition of human life, namely, consciousness, in contrast to the brain, can never become a subject of study like matter and its derivatives, and a new way of approach is necessary to fathom its nature and laws. This approach cannot be made through the intellect. It must be made by consciousness itself through methods of introspection and meditation devised in the past. Only a thin margin now remains in the recognition by science of the hard truth that all mystical literature provides the first rudimentary data of inner exploration and that it, too, will have to tread the same Path that was traversed by the mystics of old in a more rational way.

The exploration of mind, at the present stage of our knowledge, is no less difficult and hazardous than the exploration of distant planets in space. Some idea of the labor involved for attuning the body-mind instrument to higher levels of awareness, until one life is seen pervading the universe, can be framed from the labor involved in gaining world championship in a strenuous physical sport. In addition to the labor, a favorable heredity and Grace are two other indispensable factors needed for success. This position stands clearly recognized in the Yogic tradition of India from the earliest times. A complete remodeling of the cerebrospinal system in its deepest layers, like the adding of new layers of muscles to the body of a champion athlete, is necessary before human consciousness can penetrate to regions that are beyond its reach at present.

Lack of proper appreciation of this one point has led to the paradoxical position that everyone, with some knowledge of the subject and a workable command over language, writing about mystical ecstasy, believes himself to be an authority, especially if his treatise contains a heavy dose of high-sounding scientific and technical terms. This lends to the work a weight before which the reviewers and critics bend their knees. The fact is generally overlooked that the unitive state represents an excursion into a territory totally foreign to the intellect. Academic discussion of the condition and actual knowledge of it are two different things. For a scientist, who has no experience of the state himself, to write about mystical ecstasy is like a botanist who has never applied his eye to a telescope, writing about astronomy. The reason why mysticism is treated as a sort of "no man's land" is not hard to understand. There is absence of accurate knowledge and lack of unanimity in the writings about the state itself.

It is fairly well known that the most accomplished yogi and the greatest mystic ever born could not find the words to make their amazing experience in another plane of consciousness intelligible to others. They appeared incoherent as a language designed for normal experience cannot serve as a vehicle for the expression of what is entirely beyond its province. A sixteenth century erudite scholar reading a modern standard work on any science subject would find himself completely at a loss to understand it. Every branch of science has coined new words and phrases to express new ideas and concepts and to keep pace with the new knowledge gained. It is not hard to imagine what would be the state of physics or chemistry if all names and terms coined during the last three centuries were to be discarded and an effort made to compile modern treatises exclusively in the language in use before this period. Mystical experience is a profound subject and, unless it is treated as a special branch of science and teams of savants dedicate themselves to its study and first-hand experimentation, it will continue to be a disputed territory as it is now. The first thing to be done is to prepare a ground plan, a field theory and a new terminology on the basis of the material already before us. Only after this, academic debates and exploration should start.

The average reader of books on Yoga or occultism wants either to gain knowledge of the territory covered, forces involved or insight into methods by which the state can be reached with the minimum effort. The volume of literature on mystical ecstasy in India alone, dating from Vedic times, is so vast that a lifetime is too short a period to wade through it. If to this is added the mass of books from the pens of Christian mystics, Sufis, Taoists and others the load becomes too heavy for the human brain to digest and assimilate. But every year scores of new volumes, mostly from the uninitiated, are heaped on the existing mammoth store, adding to the already prevailing confusion and chaos about a subject as old as the recorded history of mankind. In this age of reason what the scholar and the lay seeker should have in mind is: what are the common factors underlying mystical ecstasy and occult powers? Is ecstasy really an encounter with God? If not, what is the nature of the experience and what forces are involved? What is the relationship between mystical ecstasy and other religious and paranormal phenomena?

Space does not permit me to describe in detail what fantastic notions about the transcendental and the occult are still held, not only by average seekers but even the learned, in a field of study that was already fairly advanced when the first pyramids were built in Egypt. It is an amazing position. There are as many views about these extraordinary or paranormal states of the human mind as there are occultists, gurus, teachers, mediums, clairvoyants, as also writers on and investigators of these phenomena. There is no single subject on which mankind stands divided to such an extent at the moment, not even excluding politics, as the science of the soul. This leaves the field open for the clever charlatan and even the do-nothing to utilize the prevailing confusion to their advantage.

Something has to be done to bring order into this confusion. Something to rescue millions from the clutches of impostors, mountebanks, frauds, opportunists and blood-suckers. There are thousands suffering from the pernicious effects of quack methods and fake disciplines prescribed by self-styled experts, and millions repenting the loss of many precious years of their life in a search that brought them nothing. The time has come when the administrations, the media and the academicians should wake up to the realization that the quest for the transcendental and the occult is as deep-rooted an instinct in the human psyche as other basic instincts and must be provided for in the same sane and healthy way as the instinct of hunger, sleep, survival and the like. This can only be possible when teams of experts are set up to make the whole province of Yoga, occultism and mystical ecstasy a subject of study and experiment as thoroughly as any other province of research.

SEVEN LEVELS OF CONSCIOUSNESS

The reason why I am particular on this issue is that there already is a huge mass of material in existence, the harvest of experiences of a galaxy stretching back to a period thousands of years before the birth of Christ. The stars of this constellation appeared only at rare intervals and their utterances are of utmost importance for humanity. For reasons which the research, in due course, will bring to light their appearance during the past two or three hundred years, despite the glamorous advance of science, has been even rarer. What is now being added to this hoary store of knowledge and, sometimes avidly devoured by millions, is superficial compared to what is already on record. It would save the writers and the readers from great loss of time and energy if, instead of running in search of fresh adventure, they were to make a thorough assessment first of what has been achieved by legions who hungered for the same experience throughout the past and made even greater effort and sacrifice to gain the same ends.

In almost every regional language of India there is a precious treasure from the past which needs digging up for a systematic study of the paranormal phenomena of mind. It must be understood that mystical ecstasy is not one thing, extrasensory perception another, psychic faculties a third and miraculous or occult powers a fourth. But they all spring from a changed pattern of *prana* or Life-Energy which forms a still undetermined force of creation. The investigation directed to study this amazing stuff will need all the resources of science, all the powers of the intellect and all the will and strength of man to learn even the rudiments. This is the reason for the attitude of utter submission before this power evinced throughout in Panchastavi.

The harvest of this investigation will be beyond anything conceived of by any thinker of standing or dreamed of by science. Even the preliminary data gathered will revolutionize the life and thinking of mankind. It will be found that the human brain stands already stamped by nature for a performance of an extraordinary kind of which there is not the slightest inkling or even a suspicion at present. This is the reason why I feel that the idea spread by the so-called yoga-adepts or the views expressed by the contemporary writers on mysticism and the occult, instead of helping to understand the mighty secret underlying the phenomena are merely adding to the chaos prevailing here. There is no one alive who knows more about this hitherto jealously guarded province as the author of Panchastavi or of any other standard work on the science of Kundalini.

There is no book by a modern author that tries to answer these fundamental questions about a province in which false pretense, deception and fraud have been a recurrent feature from the earliest times. Seemingly supernatural phenomena were caused by the priests in ancient Egypt, including the one which overawed Alexander the Great, by pure mechanical contrivances. The occultists and even the priests of other faiths seldom missed an opportunity to instill the awe of the supernatural or an irrational fear of God by artificial means whenever it suited their purpose to do so and an opportunity presented itself for doing it. False prophets and fake godmen have been and are more numerous and even more prosperous for a time than the illuminati, the real saint and the true servant of God. Save for a few honorable exceptions, the whole gallery of performers in the field of psychic phenomena is filled by those found guilty of fraud and imposture at one time or the other. The duplication by the professional magician, James Randi, of the feats performed by Uri Geller in Birbeck College, London, before keen-eyed scientists under the same conditions, has created serious doubts about his other psychokinetic performances also.[16]

How can we separate truth from falsehood and fact from fiction in a realm in which both are found inextricably mixed up from the hoary past? The mixture lends support to the believer and the skeptic both. How can unity be brought to a department of knowledge in which the world stands divided at present? Can amateur contributions lead to clarification in a branch of study in which the highest specialists, known to mankind as prophets and seers, failed to shed enough light to put their experiences and the phenomena beyond dispute? Is it too hard for our intellect to accept the position that there are still unknown momentous secrets of nature relating to mind which await discovery, and still unknown mechanisms in the human body which can radically alter the performance of the brain?

In a recent article under the title "Seven Levels of Consciousness," Joseph Campbell has tried to throw light on the ancient concept of Kundalini. His attempt has been to dovetail the hoary tradition with the modern concepts in psychology and to interpret the symbols used for the first four chakras with the views expressed by the three well-known psychologists Freud, Adler and Jung.

> "In this first chakra," he writes, "the spiritual energy is at its lowest intensity, for it is blocked from rising by the serpent's sleep. A person who functions at this level takes a grimly materialistic view of the world, one governed only by 'hard facts.' Such a person's art remains sentimental and materialistic, while his psychology might be characterized as behavioristic-reactive, rather than creative. He takes no joy in life, makes no effort to

expand. He hangs on to existence with a dull, lethargic avidity . . . . It is this lethargy, according to Kundalini Yoga, that must be cracked, so that energy may ascend into higher centers of transformation. Chakra one has parallels with the dragon-slaying myths of many cultures, including our own. The greedy dragon always hoards the greatest treasure." [17]

The view expressed is, no doubt, ingenious, but far from the truth when assessed in the light of the ancient tradition about Kundalini. Spiritual energy is not at its lowest intensity at this chakra. On the other hand the position is exactly the reverse. It is precisely at this place that spiritual energy is at its highest intensity. There is not even a suspicion in the modern works on psychology of the store of psychic dynamite existing there. The awakening of the Serpent Power can be likened to the applying of a lighted match to a powder-keg resulting in a virtual explosion in consciousness. It is thus evident that the real significance of what the Indian treatises on Kundalini Shakti, like Panchastavi, intend to convey is not correctly understood in the West.

The reason why this first or lowest chakra is called Muladhara or the 'root-support' center is because it is from this place that the explosive energy that causes the upheaval in the mind ascends to the brain in the form of a radiation and a subtle organic essence which in all books on Kundalini is designated as 'amrita' or nectar. The symbol of Kundalini, as a serpent, lying asleep at this chakra, closing with her mouth the 'Door to Brahma', is aimed to convey a hint of the untamable nature of the lightning-like force lying dormant here. Freud's 'libido' approaches close to the concept of Kundalini. But he had no awareness of the tremendous potential present in the force nor that it has a definite psychosomatic character, which was known from very ancient times.

The nature of the organic fuel responsible for the intelligent activity of the cerebrospinal system is still a distant frontier of current science. There is no equivalent for *prana* in its vocabulary. It is the change in *prana*, effected on the arousal of the Serpent Power, that causes the amazing alteration in consciousness and results in the mind-shattering experience of mystical ecstasy with miraculous powers and psychic gifts. Where in the books on psychology is there even a mention of this 'force'? The real experience of Yoga belongs to a region that has still to be mapped by science.

In the light of these facts it is not clear what Campbell means by the term 'spiritual energy' which, he says, is at its lowest intensity in the first chakra. Has he used the word 'energy' in a metaphorical sense or in the sense of the vacuous Freudian libido? If an actual force is implied, then he comes close to the concept of the Indian adepts. Then only one step remains between him and the latter. Their position is that this 'energy' can be manipulated to cause incredible alterations in consciousness and that the 'mechanism' for doing so is Kundalini.

The shift from materialism to mentalism, now gaining ground among scientists, still leaves the question unanswered: Is there a mind or spiritual energy? If so, how does it work? What is its relationship with the body? How are psychic phenomena caused? What lies behind telepathy, clairvoyance and precognition? What is behind insanity and neurosis? The 'libido' of Freud, the 'urge to power' of Adler and the 'unconscious' of Jung, in order to be effective in radically changing mental behavior, from normalcy to disorder and from mediocrity to exceptional, cannot be mere figures of speech, or but ghostly, unsubstantial abstractions, to cause serious psychosomatic diseases and those horrible distortions of the mind which defy all the efforts of psychiatrists to cure. There must be a hidden agent in the mind-brain or mind-body relationship which science has not been able to locate so far. There must be something that is totally invisible and inexplicable to us to which the still unexplained mystery of organic life is due. What modern brain experts still fail to trace must be an extremely elusive principle, so subtle and complex that a further advance in the science of life is necessary before it can be discovered and determined.

We cannot blame Joseph Campbell or any other psychologist for stopping dead at a crucial point in their study of mind and human behavior. They stand on the brink of an abyss beyond which not a single step is possible by the path provided by the intellect. They have no awareness of how the mind-neuronic interaction comes about. Taking into account the amazing advance in knowledge, achieved during recent times, we cannot suppose that our intelligence has reached the end of its tether and that the riddle of mind-brain interaction will remain unsolved forever. The solution will be found one day. The tragedy is that, ignoring this serious gap in their knowledge, contemporary psychologists have built up a huge structure without first addressing themselves to the task of determining how immaterial mind acts on the body and the latter on the mind. Do they believe that there is no such intermediary or, perhaps, that no such intermediary will ever be found? But if the nature of the 'link' is at last determined and it is found to be something which they had never bargained for, then what would be the fate of the tall, lavishly decorated, but hollow edifices built by them?

The ideas I am expressing appear implausible to skeptical scientists because they have become too accustomed to ignoring this wide gulf in their own knowledge. They do not know that the territory of Yoga begins where the boundary of modern psychology ends. The explanation offered by Campbell to correlate the theories of Freud, Adler and Jung with the ancient symbolic representations at the second, third and fourth chakras on the spinal axis are not based on a correct appraisal of the position. What the ancient adepts had in view, when prescribing the symbols for each chakra, are the changes in the pattern of *prana* and consciousness as the Kundalini force moves upward from center to center. *Prana* itself is a concept lacking official recognition. It is, in fact, what neurobiologists are searching for—the link between the neuron and the mind. The term 'pranayama', repeatedly used in the manuals on Yoga, refers to the regulation or control of this mysterious element.

The amount of study and labor involved in detecting this most elusive entity and in devising methods of regulation and control with the meager and even incorrect knowledge of psychology available in those days can be better imagined than described. The experiments had not to be made on dead matter or small animals, but on the living, feeling flesh of the experimenter himself. We seldom realize what dedication, self-sacrifice and suffering of centuries have gone into the scriptural, mystical and Yogic literature of the world. What must have been the toll of life paid in the hazardous experiments till the science of Yoga was established on its present footing we have no means to know. But that the cost in life must have been enormous goes without saying.

I have discussed the views expressed by Campbell at some length because they represent the general attitude of western psychologists towards the oriental concepts of Yoga and Kundalini. For them the criterion for the acceptance of an Eastern system depends on its conformity to the ideas expressed by some leading psychologists. But no such conformity actually exists in the case of Kundalini and even Yoga. The aim of these disciplines is to reach a transcendental level of consciousness by the manipulation of *prana*, the hidden agent behind mind-brain relationships, the vital force behind all the phenomena of life. Both transcendental consciousness and *prana* are differently ideated by different people. By transcendental consciousness I do not mean transpersonal states of mind which are now discussed in psychological books and magazines. What I mean by transcendental consciousness is a highly expanded state of the mind, described in Panchastavi as Shiva-Consciousness. It is an altered state of perception, brought about by the alteration of *prana*, which will be discussed at length in another chapter of this work.

The deepest levels of the cerebrospinal system are involved in the process of illumination. The change at these levels occurs through intense meditation, devotional prayer, worship, *pranayama* with concentration, and other yogic and religious disciplines practiced from immemorial times. Campbell himself refers to the remarks of Carl Jung admitting that the methods and philosophical doctrines of Eastern thinkers working on the problem of spiritual healing "put all Western attempts along these lines into the shade". The problem is, how could this be accomplished without empirical study which is an integral part of all scientific work today? Actually, in the case of spiritual knowledge, the empirical method came into use from the very start. Even the shaman and the witchdoctor had to resort to certain disciplines and to practise certain methods to gain the uncanny powers of clairvoyance or healing exhibited by them. Oracles, priests and magi did the same. Indian spiritual men went a step farther and built up elaborate systems of psycho-physical exercises which were later labeled as Yoga. In the Vedas proper even the name 'Yoga' is not mentioned, but the spiritual experimentation was going on. It is an error to suppose that empiricism started with modern science. Actually, all original scriptural knowledge is the outcome of empirical study and investigation. Only the laboratory and the investigator were a person's own body and the person themself. That is why Panchastavi calls Kundalini 'Pure Knowledge' (IV.1), 'Spiritual Lore', 'the Tradition', 'the Supreme Secret', 'the (whole of) Knowledge' and by other such names.

The knowledge of the 'Evolutionary Ascent' as also of the 'Transcendental Heights' to be attained, is not possible with the intellect. The sooner this position is accepted by science the better it would be for the sanity, happiness and survival of the race. The extraordinary metaphysical formulations of

Indian savants mostly proceed from insights gained in *samadhi* or the absorbed state of yogic contemplation in which the world of *prana* opens to view. This is how some of the highest philosophical systems, known to mankind, and books like the Bhagavad Gita, the Yoga Vasishtha, Panchastavi, Saundarya Lahari, Adi Granth and others, dealing with the state of awareness in higher dimensions of consciousness, the forces involved and the methods to attain them, were written.

It is a mistake to suppose that the doctrine of Kundalini merely represents a metaphorical rendering of the subliminal contents of the human psyche. In the context of current notions about mind it is hard to accept that a radiant force does actually arise from the base of the spine to create a revolution in the brain. Even the admission of this one unmistakable sign of the arousal of Kundalini can prove not only a strong incentive for empiricists for a study of the phenomenon, but also serve as an index to assess the claims of those who believe that they are illuminated. A clear, unambiguous admission of this fact is made in several verses in Panchastavi:—"Located between the four-petalled and the six-petalled lotuses (Muladhara and Svadishthana), at the end of the cavity of pudenda (i.e. between the rectum and the genital organs)," it says (V.9), "coiled three times, beaming with unbounded splendor, like that of sun, fire or lightning, Thou dost first pierce the six-petalled lotus (Svadishthana), then the ten-petalled (Manipura), then the twelve-petalled (Anahata), then the sixteen-petalled (Vishuddha), and then the two-petalled (Ajna chakra on Thy way to Brahma-randhra). O Parvati, (Daughter of Himalaya), our obeisance to Thee." The verse preceding this one expresses the same idea in a different way and there are several others besides. It is obvious that we are dealing with a still obscure phenomenon to which there are thousands of unimpeachable firsthand witnesses in the historical period, but which is entirely unknown to science and only vaguely familiar to a few scholars of our day. The way to understand it does not lie in making the phenomena subject of academic debate, some for and some against, and all with no experience of the extraordinary condition, but in organizing a concerted effort to reach to the bottom by experiment and documentary research.

The state of mind attained with the arousal of the Serpent Power is not at all to be confused with the visionary states promised by professional occultists or Yoga teachers or with the abnormal and paranormal states known to psychologists. Consciousness, when fed by an awakened Kundalini, is a condition apart and must be experienced to be understood. In marks the entry into a new life, so intense, so happy and so fulfilling that the mystics of all lands went into rhapsodies describing it. Comparing this state of illumination with the experiences of professional godmen, Rumi, the famous Persian mystic writes:—"The mystic ascends to the Throne in a moment, the ascetic needs a month for one day's journey. Although for the ascetic one day is of great value, yet how should his one day be equal to fifty thousand years? In the life of the adept, every day is fifty thousand of the years of this world . . . . May Divine Favor free thee from this wayfaring. None but the royal falcon hath found the way to the King." [18]

For the mystic himself absolute conviction of his own transformation comes not only from the vision of the Glory perceived within, but also from the knowledge that spontaneously wells up from the depths of his transmogrified consciousness. "O Mother, how can they attain Seership," says Panchastavi (I.7), "who do not learn to meditate on Thee, holding a rosary in Thy right and the book (of wisdom) in Thy left hand, with one soft hand raised to grant boons and (the other) to dispel fear, shining like white camphor and Kumuda flowers, looking with bewitching glances from Thy lovely eyes (shaped) like the petal of a full-blown lotus." This fact is mentioned repeatedly in the books on Shri Vidya, namely, the infusion of transcendental knowledge, bloom of the intellect and psychic gifts.

Can this transmutation of mental faculties, this elevation of the soul and this rich fertility of the intellect denote only a 'psychological state' without a far-reaching change down to the roots of the living organism or down to those subtle levels where Life-Energy functions to fashion us as we are? The same transformation is mentioned by Rumi:—"The spiritual man's knowledge bears him aloft, the sensual man's knowledge is a burden. God hath said: 'Like an ass laden with books; heavy is the knowledge that is not inspired by Him' . . . . Would you rise beyond name and letter, make yourself entirely pure, and behold in your own heart all the knowledge of the prophets, without book, without learning, without preceptor?" [18]

When reading the impassioned language of the mystics or books like *Masnavi* of Rumi, the erudite cynic glancing at it condescendingly not unoften thinks that he knows all about it, labeling the whole story in his overcrowded and often biased mind as 'fantasy', 'idee-fixe', 'delusion', 'superstition', 'archetypal imagery', 'subconscious fantasies', 'automatism', 'suppressed sex', or whatever comes to his memory. He is never prepared to accept that the writer has tasted the intoxicating wine of a new, sublime life, gained a new channel of perception, found another avenue of knowledge and has risen far ahead of him on the scale of evolution. He can never believe that in about a quarter of a century the subject at which he looks now so superciliously would have smashed all the records of the great discoveries made in recent times, created unprecedented enthusiasm and fervor, caused the collapse of many theories and proud notions of science and found its way to the top of all knowledge possessed by mankind at present. I envision this as only a thin strip remaining now between the last boundary of science and the wonder-stuff behind the phenomena of religion and the occult, as also of life and consciousness in man.

SCIENCE AND INDIAN PHILOSOPHY

To show how diametrically opposed the Indian philosophical view is to the current concepts of science we can do no better than repeat here the ideas expressed by Carl Sagan, a well-known astronomer, recently on the television:

"Fifteen billion years ago," he said, "the universe was without form. There were no galaxies, stars or planets. There was no life. There was darkness everywhere. The Big Bang had passed, and the explosion was rumbling down the corridors of space. The universe was hydrogen and helium and emptiness . . . Here and there in the dark, somewhat more than the ordinary amount of hydrogen and helium accidentally collected. Such clumps grew at the expense of their surroundings, gravitationally attracting larger amounts of gas . . . . As these clumps grew in mass, their denser parts, governed by the inexorable laws of gravitation and conservation of angular momentum, contracted and compacted, spinning faster and faster. Within these pinwheels of gas, smaller clumps of greater density condensed out, shattering into billions of gas balls."

"Compaction led to violent collision of the atoms at the centers of these balls, and from the simple hydrogen gas the next atom in complexity, helium, was formed. In the synthesis of one helium atom from four hydrogen atoms, there is some excess energy left over. This energy, trickling out through the gas balls, reached the surface and was radiated into space. The gas ball had turned on. The first star was formed. There was light. But since there were no planets to receive the light, there were no life forms to admire the brand-new radiance of the heavens . . . . The conversion of hydrogen to helium could not continue indefinitely. When all the hydrogen was consumed, the fires of the stars collapsed. Temperatures got so high the helium atoms themselves became fuel.

Helium was converted to carbon, carbon to oxygen, and magnesium, oxygen to neon, magnesium to silicon, silicon to sulfur . . . and upward through the litany of the periodic table — a massive stellar alchemy . . . . As these stars formed, smaller condensations formed near them — they were dense little clots, comparatively cold and slow to take shape. These unprepossessing clumps of stellar matter became the planets."

Describing the birth and evolution of life he said: - "After a time the oceans achieved the consistency of a warm dilute broth. Among all the complex organic molecules forming and dissipating in the broth, there one day arose a molecule able crudely to make copies. A self-replicating mòlecule . . . . Sex and death, the two great accelerators of the rate of natural selection, evolved. Some of the organisms subject to sex and death evolved hard parts and climbed onto and survived on the land. Flight evolved. Enormous four-legged beasts thundered across the steaming jungles. Small beasts emerged, born alive, instead of in hard-shelled containers. They survived through swiftness and running and postpartum knowledge derived from parents and experience . . . . And then came a creature whose genetic material was in no way different from the self-replicating molecular collectives of any of the other organisms on this planet, which he called Earth. But he was able to ponder the mystery of his origins, the strange and tortuous path by which he had come from star-stuff. He was the matter of the cosmos contemplating himself . . ." [19]

I am not concerned with the issue of whether the 'Big Bang' theory correctly explains the formation of stars and planets. There are astronomers who do not subscribe to this view and there are eminent biologists who have other ideas on the evolution of life. For instance, Dr. J.V. Narikar, another noted cosmologist, questions the validity of the Big Bang theory on the ground that there is too much scatter in the data on angular sizes (for radio sources) to justify an unequivocal conclusion. To be able to assert, he says, that there was a big bang the astronomer must be able to look back in time to the epoch close to the big bang. But none of the existing surveys has done that. Therefore the conclusion that the universe began with a bang is questionable since it implies the extrapolation of what we observe to limits well beyond the present range of our telescopes.

In the words of Dr. Walter Bande, another reputed astronomer, the study of astronomy should bring it home to us how little we know and how large the gaps are. Looking at the panorama of the past, it is easy to imagine that speculative accounts of creation, offered at any time, appeared like fairy tales to future generations whose knowledge of the cosmos grew more advanced. It can be safely presumed that the same will be the case with the theories floated now. The search of the intellect can never reach the end even during the whole span of the life of mankind.

What I intend to bring out here is that the Vedanta and the Shaiva systems of philosophy present an entirely different picture of the cosmos and man. According to them it is not "the matter of the cosmos contemplating itself" in man, as maintained by Sagan, but Divinity itself acting both as the Knower and the Known or, in other words, both as man and the cosmos which he beholds. It is not matter but a stupendous, incredible, unimaginable Universal Consciousness which is behind this whole colossal Drama of Creation. We are prone to err in our assessment of the power of mind as we cannot conceive of an Almighty, Omniscient and Omnipresent Mind whose mere creative thought can transform itself into a universe extended infinitely in time and space. But this is exactly what the Vedanta and Shaiva philosophies inculcate.

"When I was a student," says Heinrich Zimmer, "the term Indian philosophy was usually regarded as self-contradictory, a *contradicto in adjecto,* comparable to such an absurdity as 'wooden steel'. Indian philosophy was something that simply did not exist, like a 'mare's nest' or, as Hindu logicians say, "like the horns of a hare', or 'the son of a barren woman' . . . . In his philosophy of religion and philosophy of history Hegel coined certain formulae that are still unsurpassed for the study of history, and have been corroborated by our most recent knowledge of facts and sources (which is vastly more than what was available to him). Second to none in his intuitive grasp, he yet banished India and China, together with their philosophies, from the principal chapters of his thought, regarding the achievements of those almost unknown civilizations as a kind of prelude to the rise of the curtain on 'real' history . . . . Western philosophy has become the guardian angel of right (i.e. unprejudiced, critical) thinking. It has earned this position through its repeated contacts with, and unwavering loyalty to, the progressive methods of thought in the sciences. And it will support its champion even though the end may be destruction of all traditional values whatsoever in society, religion and philosophy. The nineteenth-century thinkers who declined to accept Indian philosophy on the par level did so because they felt responsible to the truth of modern science."[20]

The position is not much different today. The Old Guards of rationalism still hold stoutly to their guns. But a change is in the air. Whatever the scientists themselves believe, a revolt against the established schools and values is gathering momentum. There are defectors among the ranks of positivists themselves. The Riddle of the Universe is not explainable in such easy terms as scientists, like Sagan, would have us believe. There are dents in their armor which they refuse to acknowledge. Acceptance of the metaphysical systems of India implies negation of the world presented by the senses and the conclusions drawn by the intellect. This is a position entirely unacceptable to reason. The concrete structure built up by science on the basis of meticulously observed phenomena, tested time after time, of which the amazing products are before our eyes, stands out as a bulwark for the defense of reason which no power can demolish. There is no irrefutable evidence to support the idea that consciousness survives the death of the body. On the other hand, the mind of man occupies such a frail and insignificant position before the unbounded power and immeasurable dimensions of the objective universe as to be almost negligible. A contrary view which reverses the relative position of the two, from the angle of logic, cannot be the product of impartial judgement and balanced thought.

An eminent figure among the rationalists, Bertrand Russell, cites a passage from Sir James Jeans which sums up the position thus:

"The three centuries that have elapsed since Giordano Bruno suffered martyrdom for believing in the plurality of worlds have changed our conception of the universe almost beyond description, but they have not brought us appreciably nearer to understanding the relation of life to the universe. We can still only guess as to the meaning of this life which, to all appearances, is so rare. Is it the final climax towards which the whole creation moves, for which millions of millions of years of transformation of matter in uninhabited stars and nebulae and of the waste of radiation in desert space, have been only an incredibly extravagant preparation? Or is it a mere accidental and possibly quite unimportant by-product of natural processes, which have some other and more stupendous end in view? Or, to glance at a still more modest line of thought, must we regard it as something of the nature of a disease, which affects matter in its old age, when it has lost the high temperature and the capacity for generating high-frequency radiation with which younger and more vigorous matter would at once destroy life? Or, throwing humility aside, shall we venture to imagine that it is the only reality, which creates, instead of being created by, the colossal masses of stars and nebulae and the almost inconceivably long vistas of astronomical time?"[21]

Commenting on this summary, Bertrand Russell writes:

"This, I think, states the alternatives, as presented by science, fairly and without bias. The last possibility, that mind is the only reality, and that the spaces and times of astronomy are created by it, is one for which, logically, there is much to be said. But those who adopt it, in the hope of escaping from depressing conclusions, do not quite realize what it entails. Everything that I know directly is part of my 'mind', and the inferences by which I arrive at the existence of other things are by no means conclusive. It may be, therefore, that nothing exists except my mind. In that case, when I die the universe will go out. But if I am going to admit minds other than my own, I must admit the whole astronomical universe, since the evidence is exactly equally strong in both cases. Jean's last alternative, therefore, is not the comfortable theory that other people's minds exist, though not their bodies, it is the theory that I am alone in an empty universe, inventing the human race, the geological ages of the earth, the sun and nebulae, out of my own fertile imagination. Against this theory there is, so far as I know, no valid logical argument, but against any other form of the doctrine that mind is the only reality there is the fact that our evidence for other people's minds is derived by inference from our evidence for their bodies. Other people, therefore, if they have minds, have bodies; oneself alone may possibly be a disembodied mind, but only if oneself alone exists." [21]

Russell's argument is valid against individual minds, but not against 'mind' as a Cosmic Reality. An eternally existent Cosmic Mind with illimitable Power and Intelligence can create the universe with astronomical times and distances as we observe them. The evolution of life through geological ages and all the infinite variety of life forms can present no problem to an Omnipotent Creative Consciousness. The error lies in framing a picture of the Cosmic Mind on the pattern of human awareness and intelligence. Russell, as a specimen of the scientific approach, is right in his view to the extent that there is absolutely no evidence and no example of an all-powerful mind, superior to that of man, and immune to decay and death. The philosophical concept to be framed must, therefore, be based on the position actually before us. But, apart from mind, there is no proof for the existence of the universe of matter also. Of every concept framed of the cosmos and every theory advanced about its origin and evolution, mind is always an inseparable part of the picture.

The main Indian metaphysical systems are based primarily on the pronouncements of the *shruti*, i.e., the revealed scriptures — the Vedas and the Upanishads. Shankaracharya and other philosophers always fortify their arguments from this source. In the realm of transcendental knowledge their validity, for them, as the final authority is beyond dispute. This is what Zimmer implies here:

"Indian philosophy, on the contrary, has remained traditional, supported and refreshed not by outward-directed experiment, but by the inward-turned expériences of Yoga practice, it has interpreted rather than destroyed inherited belief, and in turn been both interpreted and corrected by the forces of religion. Philosophy and religion differ in India on certain points, but there has never been a dissolving, overall attack from the representatives of pure criticism against the immemorial stronghold of popular belief. In the end the two establishments have reinforced each other, so that in each may be found characteristics which in Europe we should attribute only to its opposite. This is why the professors in our universities who for so long were reluctant to dignify Indian thinking about our everlasting human problems with the Greek and Western title 'Philosophy' were far from being unjustified. Nevertheless — and this is what I hope to be able to show — there exists and has existed in India what is indeed a real philosophy, as bold and as breathtaking an adventure as anything ever hazarded in the Western world . . ." [20]

What is 'breathtaking' in the Monistic systems of Indian philosophy — which probably Zimmer intuitively grasped — is something of which science has no knowledge yet and about which it has been extremely suspicious all along. This philosophy has been mainly built on the experiences of Yoga *samadhi*, a term which, to many thinkers of the nineteenth century, betokened a singularly delusive state of mind proceeding from auto-hypnosis. Even a wide-awake psychologist, like Jung, with all his experience of psychic phenomena, classified these experiences as flotsam rising up from the unconscious. There has been absolutely no awareness of the fact that the experience of *samadhi*, when genuine, represents the ascension to a new dimension of consciousness which is the target of the evolutionary processes still active in the human brain. The relationship between mind, brain and the cosmos, which rationalism has not been able to determine yet by the circuitous route of the intellect, is revealed in this condition of highly enhanced perception with a startling clarity in which no doubt is possible. In other words, what I mean to assert is that mind itself possesses another channel of observation, apart from the intellect, by which the Riddle of the Universe can be more readily solved and this channel comes into operation in the mystical state of *samadhi*.

THE LIMITATIONS OF THE INTELLECT

Intellect is the instrument for the study and observation of the phenomena of nature, for drawing inferences from them for the discovery of natural laws and forces and for harnessing the knowledge gained for pragmatic purposes, but it is incapable of dealing with the ultimates. If such were not the case and it were possible for intellect to fathom every mystery, then there would exist no necessity for another transformation of consciousness to know the ineffable. In that case the gift of mystical vision would be a redundant possession, a duplicate instrument for the same purpose, against the principle of economy exercised by nature in the award of other faculties. The unitive experience of the mystics, on the other hand, provides an antidote to the plurality observed by the intellect, showing that two different interpretations are possible of the same phenomenon, in two different states of the same individual — plurality in one and unity in the other.

The belief in the plurality of worlds since the Copernican revolution which, in the words of Jeans, "has changed our conception of the universe almost beyond description" is not the last step in the solution of the mystery of creation. To this is to be added what may now appear to be a fantastic proposition — that the perception of this multiple creation can vary with every change in the perceptive instrument of the observer. Besides the plurality of worlds, there can be a plurality of the cognitive instruments also of which intellect is but one. According to this premise it is conceivable that earth alone is not the cradle of a species of life, capable of intelligently studying the universe and interpreting its observation in a certain manner. There may well be other life forms, too, whose instruments of perception reveal an entirely different world which they interpret in their own peculiar way. In other words, like the multiplicity of worlds there can be a multiplicity of observing intelligences also.

The gradation of the terrestrial mind, from the faint glimmer of sentience in the cell to the intelligence of man, might be but a miniature replica of the position actually existing in the cosmos. There might well be an infinitely varied spectrum of consciousness and an enormously varied scale, from the faintest to the brightest, for each color of the spectrum, spread over all the galaxies. The whole organic kingdom of earth would thus represent but one out of a vast world of colors with its varied scale of shades from plant life to humanity.

This uniqueness of Indian metaphysics lies in making this position clear to the intellect. The creation in which we find ourselves need not merely constitute the stellar and the planetary universe, on the one side, and mind, as we know it, on the other. It can be an Infinity of whose countless facets but one is presented to us by our senses and the intellect. In other words, our attempt to interpret the universe in terms of our reason might be tantamount to reducing to the position of a mellow table-lamp a mighty sun which lights up, to invest them with varied form and color, the whole multitude of objects in the solar system. What the Indian systems, Vedanta and Shaiva, aim to teach is that the Reality behind the phenomenal universe and our mind is a stupendous, incredible and unimaginable Something which can manifest Itself in countless types of creation, i.e. universes unrecognizably different from each other and from our own. The observing entities in them can also be different, with other patterns of consciousness and other channels of perception than those that feature terrestrial life. By the very constitution of our sensory equipment and mind, we cannot frame even the faintest picture of these exotic other worlds and minds however hard we may try. But our experience of dreams and, to some extent, of uncanny psychic phenomena might, perhaps, to a faint degree, suggest the possibility to which I allude. We see how the hold of reason is relaxed and how impossible situations seem natural and real in the dream state. Also how inexplicable appears to be the role of mind in precognition and psychokinetic demonstrations. A step further and other kinds of creation can swim into the area of our imagination, but the organic limitation of the brain forces us to stop dead before the frontier can be crossed.

The term Vedanta means "the end of the Vedas". The end of the Vedas signifies the knowledge gained in the *turiya* or 'fourth' state of consciousness, which means the state attained in *samadhi*, or the final condition of Yoga. This, in turn, means the end of knowledge gained through the senses and the intellect. Therefore what the Vedanta argues about the cosmos is yet beyond the frontier reached by science. The centuries of labor and the prodigious sacrifice made in India in the pursuit of supernal knowledge and the exploration of inner space has not, therefore, been a wasted effort, but has gathered a precious harvest of its own. Only science has not yet reached a stage to assess the sterling value of this crop. A synthesis is necessary and the time for it has almost arrived.

As we have noticed, the world of science is slowly coming round to the view that mind has a province of its own and cannot be an epi-phenomenon born of random chemical action. It is improbable, as some astronomers suggest, that the universe is an unimaginably vast desert of burning suns and barren planets with the exception, perhaps, of some on which life might be possible. But even that life, they presume, must be of the same variety as terrestrial life, thereby allotting to mankind a unique position as the only intelligent observer of the universe. This, in turn, makes consciousness a phenomenon confined to earth in contrast to the otherwise, uninhabited and mostly lifeless worlds. Knowledge gained in *turiya* puts an end to this premature speculation which turns creation into a monstrous ocean of fire, waste and extravagance in which the only fertile niche productive of some fruit is the earth. This radical change is effected by showing that there are other facets of the universe which do not confirm but, on the other hand, negate the overall picture drawn by the senses and the intellect. The result is that a new concept of creation begins to dawn in the illuminated.

All writers on mysticism are agreed that a mystic's apperception of the underlying Reality is of a Unity in which the diversity of the sensory image is dissolved. But this vision of the Unity is not the end as is generally supposed. It but marks the beginning of a new search, the first step in the building up of a new science, as the dawn of intellect marked the beginning of the knowledge of the objective world which we possess today. The Reality cannot be so simple as we imagine. It can be neither a plurality nor a numerical Unity, as it cannot then appear both as One and Many, but something infinitely more simple and complex. In describing the transcendent nature of the Absolute, Plotinus observes:

"... the One is the engender of the All, It can itself be none of the things in the All, that is, It is not a thing. It does not possess quality or quantity. It is not an Intellectual Principle, not a soul, It is not in motion and not at rest, not in space, not in time: It is essentially of a unique form or rather of no form, since It is prior to form, as It is prior to movement and rest: all these categories hold only in the realm of existence and constitute the multiplicity characteristic of that lower realm."[22]

"Verily, in the beginning, this world was Brahman, the infinite One," says Maitri Upanishad (VI.17), "Infinite in the south, infinite in the west, infinite in the north, and above and below, infinite in every direction. For Him, indeed, east and the other directions exist not, nor across, nor below, nor above. Incomprehensible is the Supreme Self, unlimited, unborn, not to be reasoned about, unthinkable, He whose Self is space. At the dissolution of all, He alone remains awake. Thus from that space, He awakes this world which consists of thought only. By Him alone is all this meditated on and in Him it is dissolved. He is that luminous form which gives heat in the yonder sun, the wonderful light on the smokeless fire, as also the fire which digests food. For thus has it been said, He who is in the fire, and He who is here in the heart and He who is yonder in the sun — He is One. He who knows this goes to the Oneness of the One."

These citations can be multiplied to show that there is a clear, unmistakable consistency running through the utterances of mystics of all ages and climes about an experience which alters the picture of the individual and the cosmos drawn by the intellect. They try to interpret in different mental images a new state of being which is beyond what the mind is normally accustomed to. It seems, in the words of Louis Claude de Saint Martin, as if "all mystics speak the same language and come from the same country." Bertrand Russell, while admitting the weight of this remarkable unanimity in the statements of mystics, proceeds to show that their apprehension of 'reality', in contrast to 'appearance', and the negation of time is more emotional than logical, that it expresses feeling, not a fact.

In drawing this conclusion Russell forgets that it is the close identity of the world-picture in normal consciousness that makes the experience factual. It is not the experience alone but the unanimity that lends objectivity to the phenomena observed. An individual experience or discovery, not corroborated by others, even if true, would be considered to be a delusion. This is the case with the concept of Kundalini now. Basic similarity in the narratives of the mystics lends the same weight to their experience as identity of perception lends to the experiences of normal consciousness. So long as mystical experience continues to be regarded as a purely subjective phenomenon, without any relation to the organic frame of man, it will always be difficult to rescue it from this position. Then it can never receive the same Hallmark of validity as is awarded to the intellect.

It is yet to be recognized that this consistency is the outcome of a biological factor common to all mystics, present, past or future. Also, that the demonstration of this factor can cause a revolution in the concepts of science as great, if not greater, than was caused by Copernicus. Two modes of apprehension existing in the same brain, diametrically opposed to each other, one confirming and the other negating the diversity in the material universe is a phenomenon so amazing that there is nothing comparable to it in the annals of science. It is a paradox as great, as unintelligible and as self-contradictory as the languages in which all great mystics try to clothe their experience. Were mystical ecstasy only a rare occurrence, possible but to a select, peculiarly constituted few, then it can be explained on various grounds, like the one adopted by Russell. But if it is found to be a state of cognition towards which humanity is evolving, as a whole, the problem assumes a proportion which is beyond solution at present. But this is what a thorough study of the phenomenon of Kundalini is certain to bring to light, placing an enigma before the world which might tax all its intelligence and resources to solve.

The state of oneness with the objective world in *samadhi*, an experience common to mystics, unifying the multiplicity of the intellect, puts an end to the speculations on the origin of the universe, about which astronomers are prone to philosophize. How does it benefit a rational being to know, save to enhance his theoretical knowledge of the world, that a 'Big Bang' occurred fifteen billion years ago to cause the initial movement towards the creation of the stellar universe. What is of far more importance to him is to be enlightened about his own origin and nature and he wishes to know about it here and now. He has no time to look back aeons of astronomical time or forward to another similar span to find answers to the questions nearest to his heart. It would be, perhaps, instructive to ponder the paradox that among crowds of people who all share the benefits provided by science, when it comes to making a choice, by far the greater number renders more homage to spiritual teachers than to its temporal benefactors.

Adventures of the intellect began from the very dawn of reason in man and continued since then. They amuse for a time, but are never able to assuage the gnawing hunger in the soul to know itself. Whether a sudden explosive movement ever occurred in the beginning which, in the words of Carl Sagan, "rumbled down the corridors of space" we have no certain means to know. Only this we can safely presume — that other and, perhaps, more ingenious theories will be invented to explain the origin of the universe. But a real revolution will start when it is conclusively proved, after experiment, that a 'Big Bang' can occur in the brain itself. It first occurred at the birth of reason and can occur again on the arousal of Kundalini. In the latter case, it results in a state of consciousness in which the plurality created by the former is nullified. It is this explosion that will rumble down the corridors of science for ages to come.

According to the Indian tradition this dissolution of the world, created by the senses and the intellect in *samadhi* denotes a state of consciousness free from sensory illusion. Attainment of this state signifies *moksha* or liberation, for the conscious principle in man. It is thus easy to see on what extraordinary, inwardly-gathered empirical evidence the devotees of Vedanta and Shaiva are based. The most popular scripture in India, namely the Bhagavad Gita, adumbrates in no ambiguous language the methods by which this state can be attained. Panchastavi and other books on Shri Vidya and also the Tantras enunciate the biological linkages by which the condition is made possible. If in a higher state of consciousness there can occur a loss of the objectivity of the world, presented by the senses, the inference then becomes clear that this objectivity, too, is a formulation of consciousness which interpreted their impressions. Since consciousness is expressed through the brain and organic changes in the cranial matter were responsible for the emergence of the intellect, and must also be behind *turiya* or mystical consciousness, we are faced with a stupendous mystery which may take ages to explore.

Kundalini is the super-intelligent Energy behind consciousness. It is also the evolutionary mechanism which determines the capacity of the brain. The rational mind and the *turiya*-consciousness, though opposite in effect, are both its creations at the base. The profundity of the concept has been thus expressed in Panchastavi (V.31): - "That which has gone before, that which is to come after, that which is within and that without, the unbounded and the limited, the most gross and the most subtle, the manifested and the unmanifested, the open and the secret, the near and the distant, being and non-being, in these and other forms Thou, (O Goddess), art perennially seen as the Universe. It is the movement (creative activity) born of Thee at Thy command which brings the (infinitely varied) Cosmos into being." It is an incredibly mysterious Force, a stupendous Almighty Power, an utterly bewildering Magical Stuff which forms the ground of creation. To classify it merely as 'matter' and 'mind' is to oversimplify a colossal problem to suit it to the understanding of a child.

The recognition of this fact is of incalculable value for the modern world. The Mystery behind creation is not so simple that our puny intellect can fathom it. Carried away by his achievements, man believes that he is the cream of the universe. This has led to an upsurge of pride, especially among the skeptical ranks of science, which is not at all warranted by the actual position. The real goal in front of man is to know himself. Excessive preoccupation with the outer phenomena rules out the study of That from which they arise. Real achievement does not lie in making a complicated world more complex and in adding to the problems that already exist. It lies in striking a balance between the inner and the outer worlds by which harmony and peace are achieved.

We are still a long way off in understanding the colossal nature of the Riddle that faces the intellect. An ape can never understand the problems that arise in the mind of man. A primitive can never place himself in the rich, exuberant mental world of a modern intellectual. The most intelligent thinker can never picture the aspect of Reality revealed to a mystic. The Mystery grows more intriguing, profound, and sublime as we ascend the ladder. The only thing that is made manifest, when the intellect is transcended, is the deathless, all-pervasive and absolute nature of Consciousness. Treating man as "a mere speck of matter" or as "a random creation born of chemical or organic action" can never solve the mystery of existence for both the inner and the outer worlds are one.

The Indian tradition declares this to be the aim of human life. Consciousness ascending through an enormous scale of gradations must, at last, solve its mystery. This, in other words, signifies that man, in order to attain real happiness and release himself from doubt, must know himself. It is only then that he can reach the divine stature ordained for him. How this can be realized is the objective for which we have to strive. This is what Panchastavi tries to make manifest when it says (V.32): - "Just as the rays of light rising from the sun, as the gleaming sparks rising from a fire, as the drops of spray formed by obstructed waves rising from the mighty ocean, (are reabsorbed in their source), in the same way, the multitude of elements rising and rising again with their own essential (constituent) groups are helplessly forced to fall back into stillness in Thee." Paradoxical, as it may sound, it is consciousness which is the mirror and ground of the universe — a mighty Riddle beyond the intelligence of man.

4

The Nature of Reality

MYSTICAL VISION — A FORM OF GENIUS

*T*he gift of mystical vision is as inherent a faculty as any other form of genius. The only peculiarity that distinguishes it from other extraordinary faculties is that with it are associated an intense love and devotion for Divinity, a pronounced tendency towards austerity and an inordinate passion for prayer, worship and meditation, or for other psycho-physical disciplines that help the soul to come nearer to the state of union towards which it strives. The lives of mystics, whether of the East or West, ancient or modern, amply demonstrate this constitutional peculiarity. The basis for it lies in their psychosomatic construction. The biological factors that lead to this condition have never been known or even suspected thus far.

It is because of this lack of insight into the biological endowment of the illuminati that divergent views are still held about various methods to attain the state. There are occultists and spiritual teachers who sincerely believe that, in their own particular method of approach to gain transcendence, Kundalini is not involved and that illumination can be achieved in other ways also. They show no awareness of the fact that the arousal of Kundalini can be both an extremely slow, graduated process and also a rapid, lightning-like development, depending on the constitution and the methods adopted by the initiate. In the former case, there is no perception of the activity of a force in the body and the phenomenon appears to be purely psychological in nature. But actually in all cases of real enlightenment the Serpent Power is involved.

The more drastic methods, adopted in Hatha-Yoga, sometimes result in a powerful, rapid awakening of the Shakti. The symptoms described in Hatha-Yoga manuals then become easily recognizable. This is generally not the case with the more moderate practices of Raja Yoga. This is what the author of Panchastavi implies in this verse (V.34): - "The fortunate (seekers) who, by virtue of the Mercy inherent in Thy nature and (the favor of) a discerning preceptor, entering their own Path (Sushumna), are able to cleave the enshrouding darkness of the six routes (i.e. the illusory external world created by the five senses and the mind), at once know Thee directly unto the last day as their own (indwelling) illustrious Durga in the form of incomputable Compassion and Supreme bliss who maketh the body also auspicious, (so that it is able to sustain the flame of Super-Consciousness lit up by Thee)." The import of the verse is clear. "Who makes the body auspicious" clearly refers to the biological remodeling and "those who enter the Path of Sushumna" to the seekers who undertake disciplines aimed to arouse the Serpent Power.

The next verse makes the position perfectly plain. It is the Shakti which is behind all psychic gifts, all Knowledge as well as Ignorance. "O Mighty Goddess," it says, "Thou art. Shiva, Thou art Shakti, Thou the Established Doctrines, Thou the soul, Thou the initiation, Thou this (manifested universe), Thou the Siddhis (psychic gifts), like Anima and the rest (i.e. all the eight Siddhis possible to yogis), Thou the aggregate of Gunas (Sattva, Rajas and Tamas), Thou knowledge and also ignorance. Thou (verily) art all and what is beyond it. What Tattva (element) there is (O Goddess) which is apart and different from Thee, we do not perceive." Psychic gifts (*siddhis*) are held to be a necessary adjunct to success in Yoga. This shows that Kundalini is the mysterious force behind psychic phenomena. She is also behind the perplexing drama of creation and, at the same time, the illuminator who dispels the illusion. In Shakti, therefore, we stand before a Mystery which is beyond comprehension by the mind.

Both Saundarya Lahari and Panchastavi represent the highest point of a spiritual discipline, practiced from immemorial times, revolving round the activation of this dormant psychosomatic force in the body which, when aroused, tears apart the sensory veil that binds the soul to earth, lifting it to celestial regions of such surpassing glory and happiness that, lost in wonder at the stupendous transformation, and completely removed from all that belongs to the earth, it can only say, "I am Shiva," "I am Brahman," "I am the Lord."

Based on ancient usage, this is the reason why an accomplished yogi in India is addressed as 'Swami' meaning Lord, and a Sufi mystic as 'Shah' which means King. From this peak experience has sprung the very first verse of Saundarya Lahari:— "Only when united with Shakti, can Shiva earn the position to become the Overlord (of the Universe). Otherwise the God is not able even to move . . . " The same idea is expressed in Panchastavi in these words:— "O Goddess, Thou art the Shakti (Power) of Shiva (the Creator), who has the moon on His forehead. Thou art His body, the senses, the mind, the intellect, the power of action and the doer of deeds. Thou art desire, rulership and also delusion. Thou art His refuge as also the veil that hides the reality. What is there which doth not spring from Thee?"

In order to understand the significance of these two rather enigmatic verses it is necessary to have some knowledge of the basic doctrines of the Tantric philosophy.

In His macrocosmic form, Shiva is the Overlord of Creation, but in the microcosmic state He is the embodied Jiva (soul), bound by the fetters of flesh, prone to birth, growth, decay and death. From his first entry into the world to the last moment on the earth he is prey to the buffets of circumstance or fate, always in doubt about himself, about his own real nature, his beginning and his end. He sees himself as a single unit of a colossal host, lost in the immensity of the earth, striving and sweating to satisfy his needs, also the passions and ambitions smoldering in his breast, till grim death strikes him cold, putting an end to a puzzling drama which no one has found the reason for so far.

Both in the womb and at the end the highest and the mightiest share the same room and the same last embrace of fire or clammy earth, leaving only a fleeting memory of their deeds, good or bad. It seems, therefore, impossible to believe that this puny mortal, no more than a transient bubble on the boundless ocean of existence, can ever reach a state in which the colossal Universe becomes a dominion of which he is the Lord. The mere idea seems preposterous, but yet it forms the focal point of the loftiest philosophy and spiritual thought that has won a preeminent position for the sages of India among the spiritual luminaries of the earth.

"I am Brahma (the Absolute)," says one of the seers of the Upanishads. "The Light that shines in the sun shines in me also," echoes another. "This Atman (soul) of mine and Brahman (the Absolute) are one," says a third and so it has continued for thousands of years. The same idea, in different ways and under different names, has been echoed and reechoed by at least a hundred generations of illuminated sages and Yoga saints of India to this day. Those who made this, from the present-day point of view, fantastic claim invariably won the homage and the reverence of multitudes and do so even in this age.

A modern psychologist, asked for an explanation of the riddle, would, in all probability, dismiss the whole idea as the outcome of a diseased imagination, a grandiose delusion, a fantasy, the eruption of the subconscious and so forth. For him the human mind is what it is with no latent possibilities to transcend its present limitations, and from the uncertain light of a flickering candle flame to change into the brilliant shine of the noon-day sun.

Who can deny that the stand of the skeptics is, to a large measure, justified in the light of our present knowledge about mind and consciousness? So far as the corporeal position is concerned there does not exist the slightest evidence to support such an impossible claim. How can this frail creature, swayed by every gust of passion, always under the domination of his body and lusts, claim identity with the Lord of the Universe, the infinite source of the countless hosts of suns and planets—a crowd so vast that the earth with its billions of human beings is not more than a tiny pebble on an ocean bed covered with stones and boulders for miles around.

The explanation for the paradoxical position, created by these avowals about the identity of the embodied spirit and the Oversoul of the Universe, whether we call it by the name of God, Brahman, Jehovah, Allah, Shiva, or Ishvara, lies in the experience of *samadhi*, the final state of Yoga, or mystical ecstasy that has been a recurrent feature of religious experience from the earliest times. The solution for this otherwise unanswerable riddle does not lie in the province of intellect but in the still unfathomed depths of consciousness itself. The mysterious Lamp whose light reveals the Universe can, it seems, emit other kinds of beams and rays by which the whole position of the observer, i.e., the soul, and the observed, i.e., the world, can be changed.

Most of the cosmological and metaphysical concepts of the ancient Indian philosophers are based on this experience. This is a view held by even erudite scholars like

Zimmer. The very fact that *samadhi* has proved to be an *alma mater* for imparting new knowledge or for extending its former limits or for fostering rethinking about the problems of existence is a factor of such importance that it calls for immediate attention for a thorough study of the whole phenomenon. The exploration of the mystery of consciousness never had such an urgency as it has now. A little more knowledge about himself may change the whole life and the whole sphere of activity of mankind.

The present-day writings about Yoga and mysticism, whatever the intellectual acumen displayed, throw no illuminating light on the real nature of mystical experience. The terms like 'stasis', 'entasis', 'arrest of thought', 'that-ness', 'such-ness', 'cosmic consciousness', 'unitive state', 'oceanic feeling', 'dive into the subconscious', 'contact with collective consciousness', and the rest are merely linguistic symbols to portray a state which is inexpressible. The experiences studied or recorded by modern scholars are merely brief flashes, modified by constitutional factors and environment, of an altered state of the human mind which can be hazily depicted, as far as it is possible for any language to do so, only by one who has undergone the transformation himself.

No amount of intellectual exercise can draw an accurate picture of the state. It would be like the attempt of one denied sight to explain the colors of a rainbow to others, or like one who sees the rainbow and its colors to convey his impressions to a group of sightless people. This is the reason why in the Upanishads such an attempt has been likened to the condition of 'the blind leading the blind'. This is also the reason why the term 'neti, neti', (not this, not this), has been used repeatedly to emphasize the fact that the experience of *samadhi* is not anything encountered on earth or found in the universe.

This position is difficult for the ever-searching intellect to accept. It is hard for an intelligent seeker to bring himself round to the realization that the inner being of a yogi can be so transformed that all on which his own knowledge, observation and logic are based can yield place to a new plane of experience where knowledge itself seems to have an independent world of its own, divorced from the process of 'thinking' which is an unalterable feature of the human mind. He cannot believe that a new world of mind can become accessible to a human being in which the knower, the process of knowing and the known coalesce into one.

Contributions to the already existing store of knowledge about mystical ecstasy, extant today, can only be made by those who have a constant experience of its extraordinary state. I am making this statement with full responsibility, because it would come to light, sooner or later, that intellectual contribution, instead of clarifying, has added to the confusion. For any present-day investigation of the phenomenon the most prolific source of information about this extraordinary state would be found to be the inspired compositions of the illuminati of India from the Vedic times. For many decades to come modern science will have to depend on this ancient treasure for the collection of preliminary data about this phenomenon. The scholars who now rush forward with their comments and explanations about the state or methods for the induction of ecstasy only offer themselves for the ridicule of the progeny.

"Neither by Yoga, nor by Samkhya, nor by work, nor *by learning*," says Shankaracharya, "but by the realization of one's identity with Brahman is liberation possible and by no other means."[23] Mystical ecstasy is still one of the strictly guarded secrets of nature and needs the dedication, sacrifice and sweating labor of teams of honest savants to fathom it in the same way as happened in the case of other discoveries. In fact, the dedication, sacrifice and labor involved would be found to be far, far greater than was the case with the secrets of the physical world.

Modern science has still to formulate plans for the commencement of a journey of which the end will never come into sight. Viewed in the light of these facts, the assertions made by the exponents of certain new-fangled methods of meditation or the designers of biofeedback devices that, with a few minutes' daily exercise or a few hours' practice on the machine, one can attain the same mental state which took Indian yogis or Zen masters a whole life to achieve, appear childish in the extreme. Such assertions savor of the same deplorable lack of knowledge as can be ascribed to the guru who is reported to have said to his disciples that it was not on the moon that the astronauts had landed, but on a distant, still uncharted region of earth. That even in this age of reason, crowds of seekers have the same naive beliefs about transcendental experience is clear beyond doubt.

There is a vein of identity in all the huge mass of inspired compositions in India which is unmistakable. But, unfortunately, the bulk of this treasure is not available to the Western seeker after light. This precious store has been carefully preserved by devotees and disciples and is still available for study today. The number of these inspired utterances runs into thousands, couched in different languages of India. They can be easily distinguished once the basic characteristics of mystical ecstasy are clearly defined. Panchastavi forms one of the most precious gems of this treasure. It can very well serve as a sample of numerous other compositions of the same kind. They convey in different garbs, but in their own language, the impressions of Yoga-adepts in a perennial state of higher consciousness about the nature of the transformation achieved and the experience undergone in the new state. The unique and sublime nature of the experience makes these writings priceless so long as they are not replaced by others in the times to come which penetrate to regions beyond the frontiers already reached.

True Mystical Experience

The world is still not well-informed about the fact that there is a vast gulf of difference between the hallucinatory condition of the mind, induced by drugs, inert types of meditation, hysteria or hypnosis and the mystical trance, whether a born endowment or brought about by religious disciplines of any kind. Present-day psychology is entirely at sea about this condition. In order to speak with authority any psychologist, writing on mystical ecstasy, must have experienced the peak condition himself. He has to penetrate to a region where no object is familiar to him. It is this disability that makes modern writers on Yoga with a background of modern psychology turn again and again to the subconscious. They have no other, more or less, familiar ground to help them visualize what Super-consciousness means. But the fallacy of the comparison is seldom grasped. It is still to be realized that any valid treatment of mystical ecstasy represents the beginning of a new science of which the foundation has yet to be laid.

It is because the stupendous nature of *samadhi* is not correctly understood that there still exists so much confusion and conflict of views about the Transcendental. The metaphysical systems and the whole vast bulk of the Vedic, Tantric and Puranic lore of India becomes easily intelligible when the basic features of *samadhi* or ecstasy are really understood. The first change that occurs on the onset of *samadhi* is that the puny, wavering, passion-ridden human element in consciousness recedes to the background leaving the floor open for a gigantic Personality, an infinite Being or a God of unbounded proportions to occupy the whole attention of the yogi or the mystic as the case might be.

The point here arises whether the exalted nature of the personalities or objects perceived in mystical ecstasy really proceeds from an encounter with God or the Creator of the Universe or is there a transformation of the mystic's own self so that whatever he perceives in that condition assumes a sovereign position which we associate with Divinity. This is an issue of great importance for the reason that a transformation in consciousness, which can create such a revolution in the whole being of an individual, can prove to be the very boon for which the world stands in such desperate need today.

This is what Patanjali means when he says in the *Yoga Sutras*: — "Then the self (i.e. the soul) abides in itself." In one breath it seems that this Titanic manifestation is a projection of oneself, but in the second the human element comes in between to contemplate with awe and wonder a marvelous ocean of Light and Being before which the image of the whole Universe shrinks to insignificance. The Lord and the Servant now come face to face, identical yet different, united yet separate, due to the divisive effect of the body-mind complex which holds imprisoned the otherwise Everlasting Ray of the Sun of Life. This is how Lalleshwari [24] describes the Supreme Experience:

> In the last watch of moonlit night,
> Remonstrating with my wayward mind,
> I soothed my pain with the love of God,
> Gently, gently accosting myself,
> O Lalla, Lalla, Lalla;
> I woke my Love, my Lord and Master,
> In whom absorbed, my mind was cleansed
> Of its defilement by the ten.*

Samadhi, when genuine, is a breathtaking encounter with the otherwise incomprehensible intelligence behind Creation — a dive into a boundless Ocean of Consciousness where, in the words of Ramakrishna, the salt doll of the self melts in the first contact with the upper layers of the water to marvel at the immensity that still lies beyond — a hair-raising

---

* *the five organs of sense and five of action).*

experience of infinity which makes the eyes overflow and the mind swoon in bliss. It is not hard to imagine the stunning effect of such a mighty Vision on the mind of a mortal, high or low, faced with a hundred problems and uncertain of his fate every moment of life.

The staggering effect of the encounter is described by the author of the Bhagavad Gita (11.12-14) in these words: - "If the splendor of a thousand suns were to blaze out together in the sky: that might resemble the glory of that Mahatman. There Pandava (Arjuna) beheld the whole Universe, divided into manifold parts, standing in one in the body of the Deity of Deities . . . . Then Dhananjaya (Arjuna), overwhelmed with astonishment, his hair upstanding, bowed his head to the Shining One and with joined palms spake." Without the concomitant sense of overwhelming awe, wonder and joy that seize the whole being of the yogi in *samadhi*, no trans-cendental experience can be considered to be complete or real.

A penniless man, suddenly finding himself lifted to the position of the wealthiest magnate on earth with palatial mansions, airplanes, ships and billions in cash would but experience a fraction of the overwhelming impact of *samadhi*. The same would be the case if a humble laborer were to find himself elevated to the station of the ruler of a great nation overnight.

But how can this transition come about? How can one reconcile the unconditioned, infinitely majestic Reality, encountered in ecstasy, with the humdrum life he usually leads as one of the billions of human creatures that inhabit the earth? How can one, not even the master of his own body, prone to numberless physical and mental distempers against his will, harmonize the sovereign state he attains with the frailties to which he is a prey? Can it be a grandiose delusion common to insanity or is there a hidden possibility by which, in a state of altered consciousness, the soul can triumph over flesh, gain victory over space, time and death and, shining with its own glory, assume a state of power and sovereignty before which even the staggering material Universe shrinks in size?

Every revealed religious scripture of the world is the direct harvest of this devastating experience. The attempts made to explain it form the basis of the most profound metaphysical system of India. For Buddha, Mahavira or Kapila the unique experience of *samadhi* is but the unfoldment of the glory of the soul itself, possible with the help of a disciplined and righteous life, needed to gain freedom from the domination of flesh and the trammels of the senses. For the Vedic sages and the seers of the Upanishads, the springheads of Vedanta, Shaiva, Shakta and other doctrines and systems of philosophy in India, *samadhi* provides a channel for the realization of the Supreme Reality which manifests itself as the soul and also as the Universe, whether named Ishvara, Brahman, Rudra, Vishnu, or the like.

The realization is not of the same variety. For some, as for instance Shankara, the sovereign Reality, experienced in *samadhi*, and the soul are one without difference or distinction, separated by the veil of *maya* which is unexplainable. For the Shaivites the embodied soul is Shiva Himself, incarcerated in flesh and rendered weak and impotent by His creative Shakti, the Creatrix of the Universe, His own projection and a part of His own Divine Being. The Tarika system of Kashmir describes this three-fold manifestation as Shiva, Shakti and Anu (the embodied soul) or as Pati, Pashu and Pasha, i.e. the Lord, the Creature and the fetter. The fetter is the illusive veil of existence woven by the Creative Energy of the Lord. When free of the bond the Creature becomes the Lord Himself.

This is how *Yoga Vasishtha,* one of the most popular books on transcendental consciousness, describes this unique experience: - "The Muni (sage), freed from the attraction towards objects, became of the nature of Pranakasha (the

ether of prana) pervading everywhere, the substratum of the
Mundane-egg (the Universe). He was submerged, as in an
ocean of nectar in the great bliss, where the seer alone exists
without objects of sight. He reached that jnana state which
is above all, and in which nothing but Truth exists, and
became the Ocean of Eternal Jnana and the all-pervading
Absolute Consciousness."[25]

This little detail is necessary for a better understanding
of the Agamas and Shakti Shastras. Some knowledge of the
metaphysical issues involved is needed to gain an illuminating
insight into many of the verses in Panchastavi and Saundarya
Lahari. Both according to the Shaiva and Vedanta systems,
it is the supreme Reality itself which, in a state of bondage,
caused by Shakti or *maya*, acts as the Creature oblivious to
its majesty, tasting to the dregs the cup of transient earthly
pleasure, sorrow, suffering and pain. In reflecting on the
metaphysical implications of these conclusions, it has to be
always borne in mind that they are all the result of the
revolutionary experiences undergone in *samadhi* or *turiya* in
which the Jiva, freed from the bonds of the flesh, perceives
his closeness to or identity with an all-pervading, Sovereign
Intelligent Power that overshadows and outsizes all we can
conceive of the universe.

Space does not permit me to enter into detail on the
methods used to win release from the bonded state of the
Creature in order to enable him to be the Lord. These
methods, rituals and observances are described in hundreds
of books and spiritual texts in India covering a period of
thousands of years since the Vedic times. According to the
Agamas and the Shakti Shastras the release can only occur
through the reverse action of the Shakti that is the cause of
bondage of the Jiva and the existence of the world which he
sees around.

In the microscopic form the Cosmic Energy or Shakti of
Shiva, the Creatrix of the Universe, resides in the body of
the Jiva in a dormant condition at the base of the spine,

keeping him fettered until the time is ripe for his release. This viewpoint of the Tantras and the books on Shakti is of tremendous significance for the modern world. The meticulous descriptions by hundreds, even thousands, of authors, most of whom had firsthand knowledge of the processes involved, defining the exact location and the *modus-operandi* of this peculiar energy system in the human body cannot be a mere fabrication of imaginative minds, but must have roots in a reality about which modern knowledge is still in the dark.

The stand becomes all the more authentic when it is found that the doctrine is not peculiar to India, but had its ramifications in most of the vanished cultures of the past, including the Egyptian, the Cretan, the Indus Valley, the Sumerian, and the Persian cultures. The ramifications stretch to periods even prior to the Egyptian prehistory. Books like Panchastavi, Saundarya Lahari, the Tantras and the Shakti Shastras are, therefore, the living remnants of a Secret Teaching that was in vogue in the ancient world, of which only a brief knowledge is available to history. Their value, not suspected at present, will become increasingly manifest with the advance made in the modern study of the energy system in human beings, known in India as Kundalini.

It is obvious that, in order to be genuine, any visionary experience that claims an encounter with a super-earthly power or a Cosmic Intelligence, by whatever name it is called, can only result from a radically altered activity of the brain or by the operation of a yet unknown nerve mechanism responsible for this alteration. Otherwise the condition can only be classed as hysterical or hallucinatory. To hold that the human mind can take a sudden leap, independently of the brain, from one dimension of consciousness to another, basically different from the first, is to belie experience and empirical knowledge both. No ape can ever think or behave like a man, nor can a half-wit ever reason like an intellectual. The limitation imposed by the brain on intelligence and thought is decisive in determining the mental calibre of individuals. The brain of a child comes out sealed from birth. How then can a prodigious leap to transcendental levels of consciousness be possible without the active cooperation of the physical organ of thought?

The stand taken by Panchastavi is unambiguous. There is no possibility of release for the soul except with the active cooperation of Shakti or Kundalini. The dormant Life-Energy in the body must come to the rescue of the imprisoned soul. The enfettered microcosmic Shiva, held captive by the body, the senses and the mind must have Her help to secure his freedom from captivity. This is repeatedly brought out in the song.

For the modern student the complex structure of the brain and the existence of the thirteen billion-odd neurons in it, nourished by the blood, is sufficient to account for the phenomenon of consciousness. He apparently sees no need to look for hidden mechanisms which produce and supply the psychic energy responsible for all the extremely complex activity of the body as also of thought. He does not know yet what energy is used when we move our legs or flex our arms with the exercise of our will. There must be a connecting medium by which the nonmaterial act of will is translated into action in the material of the muscle, and there occurs a transference of energy from one form into another.

The ancient adepts knew better. Tried methods of introspection, developed in the course of thousands of years, especially in India and Egypt, allowed them to gain a deeper insight into the working of consciousness and a better grasp of the energy systems feeding it. The modern scholar will have to use the same or parallel methods of investigation for a long time to come to gain similar insight and knowledge of these hidden springs of life. External observation can, to some extent, confirm, but not reveal the deeper mysteries of consciousness. For that, a dive into the Ocean of Life itself is necessary.

It is only this staggering encounter that can purge the mind of man of evil passions, ego and pride and raise it to that state of perception where, for the first time, the glory of consciousness as a self-existing, eternal entity, the bedrock of creation and the imperishable Mirror in which all the Universe is reflected swims into the ken of man. The profound effect of this encounter on the passions of mind is depicted by the Bhagavad Gita in these words: - "The objects of sense, but not the relish for them, turn away from an abstemious dweller in the body, and even relish turneth away after the Supreme is seen." Supreme here refers to the experience of the Reality in *samadhi* or *turiya*. The entrancing splendor of the vision is so soul-captivating that the ravished mind, instead of running now after the temptations of earth — power, possessions or wealth, remains centered in a more alluring object than the most enticing one tasted before.

That it is the Supreme Spirit which is, in actual fact, the source of life behind the embodied Jiva is explained by Krishna to Arjuna in the Bhagavad Gita (10.20) in these words: - "I, O Gudakesha (Arjuna), am the Self seated in the heart of all beings: I am the beginning, the middle and also the end of all beings." It is the stupendous nature of this vision, when the Creature basks in the glory of the Lord, that has been responsible for all the revealed literature and religious ferment of mankind.

It is the stupendous nature of this experience that made Buddha fall silent when questioned about the Ultimate or the nature of the Soul. It is the state of Sovereignty experienced that moved the Upanishadic seers to such eloquent descriptions of the matchless glory and all-surpassing might of Brahman. It is the ascent to this Divine Splendor that granted to Mohammed the assurance that the Message he delivered was a mandate from Allah, vouchsafed to him as the chosen vehicle of the Divine Command. It is this shattering vision of the Lord which dazzled the eyes of

Moses and smote the mind of St. Paul with such force that he fell into a swoon.

It is the absolute nature of this encounter that made Christ declare, "The Kingdom of Heaven is within you," and that, "I and my Father are one," and to hold unflinchingly to all he had preached even while suffering the unbearable agony of crucifixion. It is the undying conviction of immortality, engendered by the contact, that made Al-Hallaj cry, "An-al-Haq"—I am Truth, while marching to the place of execution, undeterred by the thought of impending death. It is the sense of unbounded compassion and grace, inherent in the very nature of the overwhelming experience, that made Ramakrishna and all great mystics, both of the East and the West, weep like children when face to face with the immeasurable grandeur and supreme happiness of the encounter.

All these facets of mystical ecstasy have been graphically depicted in Panchastavi one after the other. This points to a thorough knowledge of the extraordinary state on the part of the author. The experience, though extremely rare, has certain unmistakable characteristics that always made it possible for one who had it to recognize, by their descriptions and language, the other recipient of the Grace. Without actual experience even a well-trained intellect, with an exhaustive study of the mystical literature, would find it hard to determine, from the peculiar character of the language or expression used, whether the composition is really the product of an enlightened mind.

The homage commanded by the revealed scriptures of various faiths has, in part, rested on the fact that the succeeding generations of illuminati at once recognized, in the material before them, the craftsmanship of a Higher Intelligence and the validity of the experience of the Founder. The present-day intellect, torn between doubt and the claims of false prophets or automatic writers, often repudiate the whole phenomenon as a product of imagination or the expression of subconscious impulses that have no basis in reality. This doubt can only be dispelled by a systematic study of the phenomenon and determination of the physiological changes that attend the state.

A little more nearness of the sun can set the terrestrial oceans boiling and convert the seething water into huge masses of steam to gather into hundreds of miles thick gaseous envelope round the earth, now left with no trace of life anywhere on its surface. If the sun recedes again to the same distance the clouds, converted into water, will pour down again in unbroken torrents, like a cascading waterfall, covering the whole of earth, and fill again to the brim the vast depressions left where oceans and lakes had existed before. With a still closer proximity to the sun, even earth and rocks would melt and rise as vapor to surround the fiery, melting mass. Human ingenuity has reached the stage where the same catastrophic conditions can be created artificially with nuclear weapons. One single device can, in moments, convert into gaseous clouds one whole city in which hundreds of thousands of human beings lived, thought and acted but a moment before.

How can we reconcile this stark reality with the all-surpassing sovereign nature of the Atman (soul) as expressed in the scriptural lore of India? What imperishable, mighty atom of creation resides in the frail body of man so that it can triumph over the cataclysmic events of the Universe? The ideas expressed would not appear so impossible when it is recollected that the state of *samadhi* or *turiya* implies the release of the soul from the fetters of matter and flesh. The feeble glow of individual consciousness, cut off from its close association with the body and the world, finds itself united with an unbounded, lustrous ocean of life, with a gigantic 'Knower' spread everywhere — a boundless 'I' which pervades the whole vast expanse of space. The countless cosmic hosts, the cataclysmic events of the universe, the vicissitudes of earth, death and disaster all appear like evanescent ripples on this all-containing ocean of being, conscious of its own infinite, sovereign nature and eternal existence.

There is no reason to feel incredulous at such a transition. We know very well the prodigious leap taken by the thought of man from the instinct-bound mind of an animal. Another leap — for which there is scope in the brain, and the Universe of eternal life opens to the sight of man. The condition of the individual, before the experience of *turiya*, is expressed by the author of Panchastavi in these words: ● "O Parvati (Daughter of Himalaya), this embodied conscious being (the average mortal) cognizant of his body, composed of earth, water and other elements, experiencing pleasure and pain, even though well-informed (in worldly matters), yet not versed in Thy disciplines is never able to rise above his egoistic body-consciousness." The inference is clear beyond doubt: with the arousal of Kundalini a transformation occurs in the very texture of consciousness.

The transformation is also described, stage by stage, by Panchastavi (V.20) in these words: - "Having absorbed the universe into the body (due to the shutting out of the stimuli coming from the senses), the body, too, in the heart (mind), the heart in the self (ego consciousness), the Bindu-sustained (i.e. non-dimensional) self also in the concentrated plane known as Nada (where the Cosmic sound begins to be heard), that Nada also in the sphere of Supernal knowledge and that in the sovereign state of Supreme Bliss, (O Thou Goddess) who art of the form of the mighty sky (sky-like expanded consciousness) they (Thy devotees) who apprehend Thee (in this form) are ever victorious."

The same idea is expressed succinctly in the Bhagavad Gita (5.2) thus: - "He whose self is unattached to external contacts and findeth joy in the Self, having the self harmonized with the Eternal by Yoga, enjoys imperishable bliss." This is how Lalla expresses the same idea of transition from body-consciousness to the consciousness of the

Absolute: - "Lord, I did not know who I was, nor Thou, the Supreme Lord of all. I knew only this body of mine always. The relation between Thou and me, that Thou art I and I am Thou and both are one, I did not know. (But now I know), to ask: 'Who am I,' is doubt of doubts." Does there remain the least ambiguity about the sublime experience to which this great mystic, revered by every community in Kashmir, is alluding? It is the state of union with Universal Consciousness.

"What is the use of dilating on this subject?" says Shankaracharya in *Vivekachudamani* (394). "The Jiva is no other than Brahman, this whole extended universe is Brahman itself. The *shruti* (revelation) inculcates the Brahman without a second, and it is an indubitable fact that people of enlightened minds, who know their identity with Brahman and have given up their connection with the objective world, live palpably unified with Brahman as Eternal Knowledge and Bliss." At another place he adds, "In the One Entity (Brahman) the conception of the Universe is a mere phantom. Whence can there be any diversity in That which is changeless, formless and Absolute?" All great Indian writings about 'transcendental experience' are not just fanciful narratives of a hypothetical state, but true scientific accounts of a transhuman state of consciousness which is the crowning prize of human life.

KUNDALINI AS THE CREATRIX

Why the author has poured all his heart at the feet of Shakti and offered all his adoration to Her and not to the Supreme Lord is due to causes inherent in the nature of the experience. It is the glowing Energy rising from the Muladhara into the brain which transforms the Creature into the Lord or, at least, creates a state of union in which he shares, for the time being, the glory, the beatitude and the suzerainty of the latter. When She returns to Her abode, the glorious vision fades and the Creature shrinks back to his diminutive size. For the author, therefore, the gracious instrument of liberation is the Shakti without whose favor the union could never be possible. The overpowering nature of the encounter is described by him in these words: - "O Mother, with hairs on their bodies standing on end, with tears streaming down from their eyes and with their voices quivering with emotion, those (devotees) who ceaselessly worship Thy feet in their heart, they are, indeed, blessed."

The activation of the mechanism of Kundalini, in a system attuned to its operation, is an event so remarkable, possessing such amazing features, that the effect is stunning for one witnessing it for the first time. There is such a flood of extraordinary sensations, lights and sounds and such a change in the pattern of consciousness, all so clear and distinct, that one seems to have landed in a wonderland of unmatchable splendor, beauty and bliss. The distinguishing characteristics of the activation of the power have been defined in the very first verse of Panchastavi: — "May the Goddess Tripura," it says, "who is of the nature of light and sound, shining in the forehead like the lustrous bow of Indra (i.e., the rainbow) in the crown of the head like the luminous white shine of the moon, and in the heart like the never-setting splendorous sun — may She, by means of the three mighty syllables 'Aim', 'Klim', and 'Sauh', speedily destroy all our impurities."

Inner light is a distinguishing characteristic of all genuine forms of mystical ecstasy and *samadhi*. The illuminating glory surrounding the vision of God as seen by Christian mystics, the splendor, 'Noor', emanating from Divinity in the case of Sufis, the 'circling light' of the Taoists, 'the blazing radiance of a multitude of suns' that marks the Brahman and the 'shining halo of light' round Buddha and every incarnation of Divinity known to Hindus, are all but different expressions used to designate the same phenomenon of inner illumination experienced on the entry of Kundalini into the brain.

Unearthly shine, celestial light, beaming splendor, indescribable glory, a flaming radiance, a flood of lustre, bright effulgence, such are the terms in which those who have spontaneous interludes of mystical ecstasy describe their experience. The ascent of Kundalini is the entry of a marvelous flood of light into the whole area of the mind, lending a radiancy to thought and imagination which must be experienced to be believed. This extraordinary state of illuminated consciousness is described by the author of Panchastavi in these words: — "O Bhawani: those devotees, who see Thee clearly like the crescent of the moon, shining in the forehead, lighting from its depths the sky of the mind, these wise men soon become seers and Thou grantest all desires to these discerning souls full of faith."

This inward illumination is an inalienable feature of a brain irradiated by Kundalini. The real significance of this extraordinary alteration in the very fabric of the mind is not easy to comprehend. The general impression about this peculiar feature of ecstasy is that the visions seen are bathed in lustre or that Super-earthly splendor surrounds the figures or the objects perceived in the state. Other current notions, based on the altered states of perception induced by drugs, are of scintillating bright spots, flashes or streaks of light, spiraling luminous vapors, riots of colors and lights, greater brilliancy than normal, peculiar hues, pigments and shades and the like. This is not at all what the descriptions in Panchastavi try to portray.

The actual position is that it is not the figure or the object or the landscape, seen in the altered condition, that is resplendent or has a shining halo round it or is seen with new colors and pigments or that luminous patterns float before the eyes, but that the observer is himself enveloped in a glorious mantle of light. The very fact that such notions are held, even by intelligent seekers after Transcendence, reflects a sad state of knowledge about the essential features of *samadhi* or mystical ecstasy. I am emphatic on this point because a scrutiny of this one single characteristic of transcendental consciousness can determine whether the experience is a genuine product of a properly activated Kundalini or the result of artificially induced hallucinations or delusions with drugs, self-hypnosis, suggestion or other causes.

The terms like 'the self-luminous Atman', 'the golden Purusha', 'the resplendent Brahman, Shiva or Vishnu', 'the Orient Guru (Hiranyagarba)', repeatedly used in the Vedas, the Upanishads and other scriptural lore of India are not mere euphemisms or figurative expressions, but apply to a stern reality of the highest importance to present-day mankind. There is much confusion even about the correct translation of these terms because their significance has been almost entirely lost. What the modern seekers after Yoga must know is that *prakasha* (illumination) is the first positive sign of spiritual awakening.

This inner radiancy that makes the mind glow like a sea of light is described by Saundarya Lahari (I.6) in these words: - "Such rare, high-souled men, who worship thee as Aruna, radiant as the morning sunlight, (causing) the lotus-like mind of great poets (to bloom), delight (the assembly) of wise men with their diction profound like the fresh flood of erotic Sentiments flowing from Virinchi's beloved spouse (i.e. Saraswati, the Goddess of Learning)." This is also a reference from the alleged author of the work, the great Shankara, himself a poet and philosopher of the highest eminence, about the emergence of poetic talent as one of the attributes of illuminated consciousness.

That the perceptive quality of the mind undergoes a transformation when Kundalini pierces the Ajna chakra, controlling the gateway to the brain, is clearly brought out in verse 37 of *Shat Chakra Nirupana*, thus: - "He (the yogi) also sees the Light which is in the form of a flaming lamp. It is lustrous like the clearly shining morning sun, and glows between the Sky and Earth. It is here that the Bhagvan (Lord

Shiva) manifests Himself in the fullness of His might. He knows no decay and witnesseth all, and is here as He is in the region of Fire, Moon and Sun." [26]

The yogi now, as a Creature, perceives the Lord or becomes cognizant of his own identity or unity with Him. The relationship between the observing ego in mystical ecstasy and the transfigured entity observed has been diversely interpreted by the Seers from the earliest times. This variance in interpretation has not been glossed over, but is clearly mentioned in the same work in these words: - "The Shaivas call it the abode of Shiva, the Vaishnavas call it Parama-Purusha, others again call it the place of Hari-Hara. Those who are filled with a passion for the lotus feet of the Devi (Shakti) call it the excellent abode of the Devi, and other great sages call it the pure place of Prakriti-Purusha." The profound significance of the verse is clear beyond the least shadow of doubt. If in place of the different religious sects in India, we insert the diverse major faiths of mankind — Buddhism, Islam, Hinduism, Christianity, Zionism, etc. — the conclusion then becomes clear that they represent different interpretations of the same experience arising from the entry of Kundalini into the brain.

This conflict of views about an experience, beyond the reach of the intellect, finds mention in Panchastavi (V.7) also in these words: — "O Illustrious Goddess, some there are who declare Thee to be Real (perennially Existent). There are others who call Thee Unreal (Transitory). There still are other intelligent thinkers who proclaim Thee to be Real and Unreal both. (Apart from these), there are still other wise sages who hold that Thou art neither Real nor Unreal. O Goddess, O Thou Consort of Shiva, all this is but the manifestation of Thy illusive power."

The mind of an average person, transformed all at once into the highly imaginative, artistic mind of a Michelangelo or of a great astrophysicist would find itself at sea for a long, long time before it could attune itself to the vivid imagination and the versatile genius of the former or the immense wealth of knowledge about the stellar Universe of the latter. The entry into a new world of consciousness, where reason is of little avail, is tantamount to the entry of a sightless person born blind into the world of light at a late stage in life. They must first get accustomed to what their eyes now behold for the first time.

The reason why there is so little awareness about this aspect of mystical ecstasy lies in the fact that it has all along been presumed to be an encounter with God, or the Reality behind the Universe or a Superhuman Power that initiated the ecstatic into the mysteries involved. There was no need for a long preparation or a period of training as the Divinity or Superhuman Being saw to it that the issues arising from the encounter and the secrets revealed were understood. The mere attainment of the blessed state was a sufficient guarantee of the fact that the individual had been singled out for the favor and was the chosen vessel for the knowledge imparted or the revelations made. This supposition has been one of the greatest stumbling blocks in the proper evaluation of mystical experience, and in the correct understanding of the purpose and importance of Revelation on which most of the current faiths of mankind are based.

This all-important issue will come in for detailed discussion in another work. Here it is enough to point out that if ecstasy or *samadhi*, in actual fact, represents a change in consciousness from the human to a transhuman dimension, then a period of adjustment to the new development cannot but be an essential feature of the transition. The mind would take some time to find its bearings and to familiarize itself with the terrain of the new country in which it sees itself. To ignore this contingency is to cast a doubt on the validity of the experience itself.

At the present stage, mystical ecstasy represents but the first and not the final rung of the ladder of evolution designed to lead the whole of the race to a still unknown state of consciousness. If mystical experience or *samadhi*, in actual fact, denotes ascension to a higher state of awareness and contact with transhuman planes of existence then, in a law-bound universe, there can be no room for it as an arbitrary favor confined to a selected few. It, too, must then be ruled by a universal law which is not known to us. The conflict of faiths arises from the fact that the experience has been diversely interpreted and the knowledge gained and the revelations received treated as final, beyond which it was neither necessary nor possible to reach.

ILLUMINATIVE RADIANCE AND A COSMIC SOUND

The repeated emphasis in Panchastavi and other allied treatises on luminous and acoustic phenomena, on the dawning of supernal knowledge, on the emergence of poetic talent, on inspiration and revelation which, in the usual course, are commonly met features of mystical ecstasy, all point to the operation of a new faculty or a new mode of cognition not in evidence in the normal condition. This leads to the conclusion that in a background of peculiar lights and sounds, fragments of hidden knowledge, gems of wisdom, flashes of insight and finished products of inspiration come within the field of perception of the contemplative.

"In the minds of fortunate devotees, O Mother", says Panchastavi (IV.3), "Thou dost manifest Thyself as the glowing sky (Super consciousness), as the Bindu (non-dimensional void), as Nada (the Cosmic sound), as the crescent of the moon, as the fount of expression (genius), as Mother, as the fount of Bliss and the Nectar of Jnana (supernal knowledge)." In this one single verse, all the features of mystical ecstasy, known from the earliest times, are concisely defined. The epithet 'Mother' has been frequently used as the sense of gratitude at the sovereign favor and limitless compassion involved in the boon of Transcendental Consciousness is overpowering. The whole suffering of countless lives melts away at the first encounter with the Divine. Only the extreme love of a fond mother could patiently guide an erring mortal to such a priceless treasure.

The modern exposition of the Serpent Power, in commentaries on the ancient esoteric documents, dwells mainly on the magical, miraculous and arcane aspects of the science. The extremely precious bits of knowledge, scattered here and there, that can prove of inestimable value to modern savants and seekers both are often overlooked. The subjoined verse from Panchastavi (V.21) would amply illustrate what I mean: - "O Thou, who art the Code of Conduct (in religious observances), the Repository of all Knowledge, fit to be comprehended, the Source of all Established Doctrines, the Author and the Quintessence of the Vedas, the Mine of Wonders, the Origin of the Universe, the Controlling Power of Lord Shiva, the Springhead of all Morality, the Abode of Shiva-Consciousness and the Instrument of Unity with Him, O Mother, who art (inseparable from) Shiva, easily attainable through humility, bestow on us (the boon of) unparalleled devotion to Thee."

Interpreted at its face value the verse merely reflects the warm effusion pouring from the heart of a devotee at the feet of the Goddess who, for him, holds the same sovereign position as Ishvara, God, Allah or Brahman have for those who worship them as a religious duty. But this is not the only reason for the meticulous definition of the exalted offices attributed to Shakti in this verse. There is a deeper esoteric significance which, when apprehended, throws an illuminating light on the effusion of the author. It is not merely sentimental devotion, but the basic realities of the incredible experience of Laya-Yoga *samadhi* that form the background for these lines.

Briefly stated, the ascent of Kundalini into *sahasrara* heralds the commencement of a transformation in consciousness which, in a healthy system, can continue to the last breath, opening fresher and ever fresher vistas of a glorious inner world, so far removed from all we can imagine that it never ceases to be a wonder from the first to the last. This is the reason why Shakti is addressed as 'the Mine of Wonders' in this verse. The first impact of the ascent is felt in the strange, entrancing lustre in the head and continuous music in the ears. It is for this reason that Kundalini is said to be of the nature of Light and Sound in the very first verse of Panchastavi. The Sound is variously described and its mystery diversely explained. The sacred syllable 'Aum' is said to be the greatest of mantras and the quintessence of the Vedas. Yogis in India refer to the music produced by this Sound as a self-playing Orchestra. It is prone to variation in different states of contemplation and different conditions of the body.

The luminosity in the head is a phenomenon so incredible that it is extremely hard to explain it to those who have not had the experience. As already explained, this luminosity is not observed in the same way as a light seen through mortal eyes. On the other hand, it is the observing apparatus, the thinking mind, its imagination and thought, that becomes luminous. When the transformation is complete, all thinking and all visualization is done in a mental world of light. In other words, the inner man — the thinking, willing, ego-consciousness — now wears a raiment of light and, in deeper states of contemplation, floats in a luminous, throbbing sea of life, much as an incandescent globe of gaseous matter, risen high, would be seen floating against the background of a brightly shining sky. This is why Kundalini is often likened to the 'glowing sky', to the 'starlit firmament', to the 'milky way', to the 'Moon', 'Sun', 'Fire', and 'Lightning'. The underlying idea in every case is to convey the otherwise undepictable transformation in the texture of consciousness that keeps the inner being of the accomplished yogi always ablaze with light.

It is possible that this exposition of some of the verses in Panchastavi would be considered to be an exaggeration and received with incredulity. The very nature of my assertions makes it unacceptable to the modern intellect. But there is no escape from the logical position. The descriptions which liken Kundalini to fire or lightning and the *ida* and *pingala* to the moon and sun make it abundantly clear that a luminous phenomenon is involved. In a healthy metamorphosis the effulgence is highly soothing, blissful and enrapturing, and is, therefore, compared to the lustre of the moon in the head. This is the reason for the emblem of the moon on the head of Lord Shiva and the hair of Shakti, alluded to in the work. But when the awakening is unhealthy the light becomes the blinding glare and tormenting fire of insanity.

The ultimate aim of Yoga is to cause this marvelous transformation in the inner being of the yogi. In the final stage of the change he eats, drinks, walks, acts and dreams always surrounded by a glowing world of light. The impressions coming from the outer world now wear a different aspect. The glowing consciousness imparts a radiancy to the Universe also. The senses function as before. There is absolutely no blurring or distortion in perception. Only the relationship between the Seer and the Seen is changed. The consciousness of the observer now seems to fill the whole of space. This is a marvelous experience of which the wonder, instead of diminishing with lapses of time, continues to grow.

The world presented by the senses seems to float in the observer's own lustrous ocean of being. The mind acquires a new penetrative power. The Universe no longer appears to be a gigantic creation, by its unimaginably vast size reducing the observer to a state of utter insignificance and helplessness, but, on the contrary, it now appears like an Island in a luminous Sea of Being. An element of divinity is henceforth introduced in the composition of man. He is no longer a puny creature, encased in flesh, and surrounded by a cosmos which dominates him by its size, but an eternal Ray of life, beyond birth and death, on which the body and the world around sit as phantom shades, like clouds before the face of a blazing sun.

This release from the domination of matter is described in Panchastavi (V.11) in these words: - "Shining with the brilliance of millions of suns at the time of Dissolution, with Thy splendor Thou burnest to ash the forest with the six routes (the world of illusion created by five senses and the mind) of those devotees whose heads remain bent at Thy lotus feet; making fully manifest (to them) the glory of the unparalleled Shiva with the effulgence of Thy lotus-like form, bent with the weight of breasts which, as the prowess of Shiva, is ever victorious."

It is this process of release of the soul from the thraldom of the senses that has been variously described in religious scriptures of mankind as 'Salvation', 'Mukti', 'Yoga', 'Union with Brahman or God', 'Crossing the Ocean of Illusion', 'Illumination' and the like. This experience is even more breathtaking than the experience of the inner light. The world which appears so real, concrete and colossal in the normal state, in a mysterious way, loses all these salient features and becomes itself a mere reflection of the same consciousness which is dominated before.

This astounding shift from corporeality to bulklessness is described in Panchastavi (V.15) thus: - "O Mother, how great is Thy glory that even though swallowed up by earth, water, fire, air, mind, the sun and moon (i.e. though enveloped by all these elements in the embodied Jiva), in Thy superfine state of sky-like (expanded) Consciousness, not a trace of any of these enveloping sheaths is found there." What the Shakti Shastras deal with is an advanced type of consciousness in which the senses are transcended to reveal a non-spatial and non-temporal picture of the Universe.

The only explanation that can be provided for this change in perception is that in the higher dimension of consciousness, created on the awakening of Kundalini, the mind acquires a highly penetrative X-ray quality which makes the erstwhile massive objective world seem like an illusory appearance, not real in itself but only a projection of the observer. This is the reason why Vedanta declares the Universe to be an illusion, a transformed image of Atman (soul) or Brahman itself.

This marvelous experience is common to most mystics. This is how Lalleshwari describes it: - "By oft-repeated practice, the wide expanse of manifested Universe is lifted to absorption; and the Saguna world, of forms and qualities, merges in the vastness of the Void, with a splash like water on water falling. Then the ethereal Void dissolves and the Ineffable Supreme alone remains. This, O Bhatta (Brahman), is the Truth to gain." How remote from the present-day distorted notions about Yoga does this avowal of an acknowledged adept in the science sound. The most amazing feature of accomplished Yoga is the inner revolution which turns the Universe into a melting ghost.

This is why the Upanishadic Seer declares with absolute conviction that all this is Brahman and there exists nothing besides that. This is also why the Shaiva philosophy believes the world to be a transformed form of Shakti, the creative power of Shiva or, in other words, a transformed image of Shiva Himself. On the union of Shiva and Shakti, when Kundalini illuminates the mind, the world dissolves in the flame of consciousness like a shadow dispersed by the entry of a brighter light.

This new form of cognition which seems to pervade the whole universe is not merely a transformed form of normal human consciousness operating before, but an amazing ocean of infinite wisdom and unmeasurable intelligence so concentrated that each drop contains an ocean of Knowledge within itself. This is the reason why, in the state of mystical ecstasy, there is a definite sense of enhanced awareness and deeper insight into the nature of things. Due to the limitations imposed by the brain, it may not be possible for one to bring back this experience into the normal state, but the awareness of enhanced knowledge during the trance is unmistakable.

In exceptional cases, fragments of knowledge gained in this condition filtered down as Revelation which form the seed-bed of all revealed scriptures of mankind. In the case of genius, the insight gained, the new discoveries made or the inspired material gathered all flow from the same inexhaustible ocean of the Universal mind. This is the reason why, in the verse reproduced above, Kundalini is held to be the Code of Conduct, the Repository of all knowledge, the Author of the Vedas, the Springhead of all morality and the rest, as all science, philosophy, art, ethical standards and the Revelations of religions descend from the ocean revealed by Her to become a part of Human culture and life.

The famous Vedic prayer, "From darkness lead me to Light, from the Unreal lead me to the Real, from Death lead me to Immortality," is an abbreviated version of the same transformation. The inner being of an illuminated soul embodies all these three features of transcendental life — Splendor, Reality and Freedom from the fear of Death. The same idea is beautifully expressed in Chandogya Upanishad (III.14.2) in these words: - "He who consists of mind, whose body is life (prana), whose form is light, whose conception is truth, whose Soul (Atman) is space containing all works, containing all desires, containing all odors, containing all tastes, encompassing this whole world, the Unspeaking, the Unconcerned . . . ."

The same self-luminous state of Brahman is described in Katha Upanishad (V.15) in another way: - "The sun shines not there, nor the moon and stars nor these lightnings, and much less this (earthly) fire. After Him, as He shines, everything shines, this world is illuminated with His light." The same stanza occurs in the Mundaka (II.2.10) and also in the Svetasvatara Upanishad (VI.14). A similar passage is contained in the Bhagavad Gita, too. This idea is further elaborated in the Mundaka Upanishad thus: - "In the highest golden sheath is Brahma, without stain, without parts. Brilliant is it, the light of lights — that which the knowers of the Soul (Atman) do know."

The main attempt of the Upanishads is directed at defining the extraordinary pattern of consciousness attained in the beatific state. The Maitri Upanishad (VI.35) describes it in this way: - "Of the bright power that pervades the sky it is only a portion which is, as it were, in the midst of the sun, in the eye and in fire. That is Brahma. That is the immortal. That is Splendor. That is the Eternal Real . . . . That is heat. That is breath. That is matter. That is the moon . . . That is the realm of Brahma. That is the Ocean of Light."

How alike are the features of the experience of *turiya* as contained in the Upanishads, or as described in Panchastavi. Shiva is self-luminous. So is Atman, so is Purusha, so is Brahman and so is Shakti. Each one of them is the first cause of the Universe and everything in it. Earth, water, fire, air, ether, the sun, moon, the Vedas, the mind and intellect all arise from it. The conclusion is, therefore, irresistible that all these descriptions proceed from an identical experience which has been differently interpreted by the seers who had it.

It is extremely hard for a modern down-to-earth intellectual to accept the fact that human consciousness can attain to a state of perception where the solid Universe is reduced to the position of a shadow and one Eternal Life is seen pervading the cosmos. Such an affirmation proceeding from another lofty intellect, as for instance of a Shankaracharya or Ahhinava Gupta, would at once create a doubt about their judgement of observation in his mind. But his skepticism is unwarranted, if not downright irrational, for the reason that what they are talking about involves the operation of a new form of energy about which modern science is still in the dark.

5

The Inner Universe

ALTERED STATES OF CONSCIOUSNESS

*T*he reason why the idea of a still untapped reservoir of psychic energy in the human body is often unacceptable to the intellect lies in the fact that it does not form a part of the cultural tradition of the West. The Western scholars treat body and mind either as an inseparable duality or as two interacting entities completely different from each other. The Semitic faiths inculcate the idea of a soul which, in a still undetermined way, makes the body its abode for the duration of its earthly life. There is generally no recognition of the fact that mind or ego-bound consciousness is a form of energy so subtle and complex that it is beyond the reach of our intellect.

We can never have perception of another consciousness as we have of our own, although we live surrounded by millions of fellow beings in possession of a conscious apparatus more or less like our own. But we never objectively perceive it, as we see the body, and are only aware of it by inference. But individual human consciousness is not the only form in which this energy can be met with. It is present in every nook and corner of the universe, capable of acting at the deepest levels of atoms and molecules. The awakening of Kundalini, in a harmonious system, causes a revolution in the texture of this energy with the result that a new world of perception opens before the amazed inner eye of the awakened individual.

Generations of yogis in India, for the past thousands of years, have been a witness to this amazing transformation. The record of their experience still exists in the Vedic, Puranic, Tantric and Yogic literature extant in our country. But there has been no attempt so far to integrate all these varied interpretations of the same experience and to demonstrate the identity of the basic factor that is common to them all. That factor is Kundalini.

In a modest way, in spite of my frailties, I am myself a living witness to this extraordinary phenomenon. I live, act, think and dream in a world of light. The accounts left by the great mystics and seers of the past, whether Eastern or Western, make an instant appeal to me. I live among them and they, in a sense, live in me. Every stanza of Panchastavi has a personal bearing and a hidden import for me which is not transparent to most other readers of the work. I know in what state of mind the author must have lived, and what overpowering sense of gratitude to the divine Power, responsible for his transference from the world of delusion and death to that of Reality and Eternal Life, must have prompted the song.

This transference from the world of darkness to that of light is described by Lalleshwari in several beautiful passages. In one of them she says, "I turned to Him with all my heart and soul and heard the ringing of the bell of Truth. There, in Dharana (the yogic state of concentration), fixed in thought, I soared the sky and the Regions of Light." [27] This is a clear reference to the inner sound and the inward light. The former, sometimes, resembles the soft tinkling of a musical bell, at other times the soothing murmur of a gently flowing mountain stream, at still others the humming of a swarm of bees and so on.

I have dwelt at length on this phenomenon of inner effulgence, as this is the most prominent characteristic of mystical consciousness. What the ego of the illuminated person perceives is a Splendor, sublime beyond description, dwelling in the body, still prone to hunger, thirst, sleep, fatigue, desire and passion, in a rational way but, at the same time, conscious of its own eternal substance, as if the sun had bodily descended to live in and illuminate a narrow, dark and dingy cavern on the earth.

The world stands desperately in need of a new era of spiritual revival. The present-day widespread interest in Yoga and the occult is the outer symptom of an inner urge that urgently demands a correct appraisal of its nature to avoid abuse. In a nutshell, the Divinity in man wants to assert itself. This has often happened throughout the past. Whenever a settled, organized way of life enabled any section of humanity to live in reasonable comfort and peace and to have some time to spare, an irrepressible impulse, rising from within, drove members of the community to seek answers to the Riddle of Existence, to the Mystery of Creation and their own Being. This led to the multidirectional search for the supernatural, the occult and the divine.

This elevation of the divine in man is the real aim of Yoga and of all religious disciplines and faiths of mankind. The soul must rise above the fetters of the senses to gain awareness of its own glory and eternal being. The emancipation of the divine spark, clothed in flesh, is the avowed aim of all the current major faiths of mankind. But a flood of intellectual speculation and an incorrect presentation of the real purpose of faith has created a climate of confusion and disbelief in which the real aim of spiritual discipline has been lost. The first attempt of every seeker should be to determine the goal. When this is done the methods to achieve it would not take long to find.

The most effective way to bring about the consummation is to keep this sublime end always in view. The whole life of an individual must revolve round this supreme resolve. The feeling of surrender and submission to the divine must pervade one's whole being. No amount of study, no degree of practice, no method of Yoga, no secret key to success and no esoteric discipline can tear asunder the veil and reveal the matchless glory of the Self until the right environment is created both within and without.

An aspirant can but knock at the door of salvation and continue knocking all his life. But the door has to be opened by a Superhuman Cosmic Intelligence which knows him in and out. Where, then, exists the possibility of a breakthrough until the Lord is satisfied? This is a position that is unacceptable to many who, intoxicated with pride, believe they can take even the Divine by storm. This frame of mind does no harm to Divinity, but entangles the soul deeper into the web of delusion. It is for this reason that every prophet and every mystic ever born took constant pains to place the ideal of humility and surrender to the Divine will before the seekers, as the first essential requirement of a spiritual life.

The Majesty revealed in *samadhi* or ecstasy, showing the gulf of difference between the ego-bound, conceited creature and the Lord, leaves not the slightest room for pride. This is how Panchastavi (II.27) describes the frame of mind of one humbled and chastened by the Vision seen. "O Goddess: May my eyes ever ardently seek to visualize Thy form, may both my ears ever long to listen to descriptions of Thy countless virtues, may my mind ever be engaged in Thy remembrance, may my voice be always raised in Thy praise, may my two hands ever be busy in actively worshiping Thy feet. (In short) may my zeal for worshiping Thee never diminish in any way."

And again (V.27): - "At the time when my father, mother, brother, wife, very loving friend, household, my own body, son, attendant and even wealth forsake me, at that time (of departure from this world) do thou, O Moonshine-like infinitely Glorious Mother, out of compassion dispersing the (binding) darkness of ignorance, attachment and fear, instantly manifest Thyself unto me." The purpose of the Vision of deathless Glory of the Soul is to overcome the natural and instinctive fear of death. The attitude of perennial worship of the Divine, even while engaged in the conquest of the forces of nature and the exploration of space, is as necessary for the individual as for the race to raise mankind to her sublime estate. A conceited and individualistic bent of mind has been symbolically portrayed in the religious lore of mankind in the rebellious nature of the Prince of Darkness — in the case of Semitic faiths — and in that of the Asuras in Hindu mythology.

The stress on certain syllables, like 'Aim', 'Klim', and 'Sauh', on mantras, on diagrams, or on pronouncing the letters of the Sanskrit alphabet in a certain way or their existence on the petals of the lotus to be visualized on the chakras, is in accordance with the ideas and the usages of the time when Panchastavi was composed. Otherwise, all the various manifestations connected with the arousal of Kundalini are concrete realities governed by biological laws about which we have no knowledge at present. There is nothing of superstition, myth or miracle about the phenomenon. It is miraculous in the sense that we have no knowledge of the force involved in it.

The one single characteristic that adds a supernatural or divine color to it is that the Energy behind the various strange and, sometimes, even uncanny and bizarre manifestations seems to be possessed of an intelligence which is entirely beyond our conception. We can frame a distant picture of it in this way: suppose an impregnated ovum in the womb of the mother becomes aware, as we are, of what changes take place in it during the process of growth. Imagine, then, its wonder and bewilderment, during the whole period of its embryonic life, at the storm of intelligent activity which it witnesses within itself every moment resulting, with the division and the multiplication of one single fertilized ovum, in the formation of a human infant, complete with all organs and limbs. Experience of thousands of years, with constant scrutiny and handling of the human body, has not enabled us yet to fathom its mystery or to know even a fraction of the marvels hidden in the brain — an organ so complex that there is nothing compared to it on the earth.

The difficulty with the skeptic is that, whatever be the degree of his understanding, he lacks the power to imagine the staggering dimensions of intelligence and skill needed for such an achievement. There is nothing so preposterous as to suppose that such a marvel of intelligence and skill which, mark you, transcends our intellect even to understand, could be fashioned without the direct agency of a higher intelligence far, far superior to our own.

Like one with a deficient vision for a certain color, the skeptic sees and draws his conclusions with the aid of a highly trained intellect. But the omission of that one color renders all his conclusions wrong. This is the reason why in the Indian scriptures great emphasis has been laid on *viveka*, i.e., the power of right judgement or discrimination. This is a quality which, according to Plato, must be present in a philosopher. This is also what the term *buddhi*, as used in the Bhagavad Gita, signifies. Mere book knowledge or a high degree of intelligence is not sufficient for an understanding of the mysteries of creation. They must be tinctured with wisdom and deep insight.

Present-day knowledge treats the human body and the brain as a sealed system with no room for a performance that completely transcends their normal limits. The now century-old investigation of psychical phenomena and the huge volume of evidence, gained by competent investigators, has not sufficed to open the eyes of the world to the fact that there are still depths in human consciousness and the instrument of its expression, i.e., the brain, which they have not been able to fathom so far. In many cases the blind spot in the mind that omits to see a certain 'color' is responsible for this inability. Freud's condemnation of religion shows a lack of insight and poverty of knowledge about mystical ecstasy that is astonishing.[28] What Panchastavi attempts to expound is as far away from the concepts of Freudian psychology as the landing of a Martian expedition on the earth.

It has to remembered that ascension to a higher level of consciousness, in which the divine nature of the Self becomes manifest, permitting the human soul to have a glimpse of its own glory, involves the opening of a new channel of cognition in the brain. This is what is actually meant when reference is made in Panchastavi to the entry of Kundalini into the *Brahma-randhra* to achieve the enrapturing union with Her Lord. It is here that the vivifying stream of nectar, repeatedly mentioned in the work, wells up in a mysterious way with an indescribably transporting sensation, in the brain itself, to irrigate the whole area of the cranium. In a manner which future investigation will show, this nectarean substance, culled by nerves from all parts of the body, provides the biological fuel to carry on the processes necessary to build up the new center.

The clinching evidence for the objective nature of the phenomenon of mystical ecstasy and Cosmic Consciousness will only be provided when it becomes possible for science to verify the altered activity of the nervous system, the flow of this ambrosial current into the head and the changes that occur in certain areas of the brain itself. That the phenomenon is based on a biological reality I can assert without hesitation. The denials of skeptics do not belie the Tantric tradition nor the avowals of thousands of Indian adepts, but only highlight the present deplorable poverty of knowledge about the brain. With the first rudimentary success in this investigation the stampede that will follow to hunt for bits of vital information in the Tantras and books on Shri Vidya, like Panchastavi, is not hard to envision. A time may come when the accounts left by ancient explorers

of the uncharted regions of inner space will be sought for
and read more avidly than, may be, even the first-hand
accounts of the brave spacemen who first land on one of the
distant planets, when the feat becomes possible.

Such a complete reversal in the shifting of interest from
the outer to the inner world may appear unrealistic in the
context of present-day trends. But once the all-surpassing joy
and wonder of inner exploration becomes even half as well
known as voyages in outer space, there will be nothing to
compare to the fascination exercised by it on the adventurous
spirits of every age. Then only can the greed for power and
wealth abate, and the race for armaments come to an end.
Then only can evil, crime and violence subside, for a new
horizon, a new ideal to strive for, a new vision of the universe
and a new springhead of lasting happiness will then open
before the eyes of the seeking crowds.

The modern writings on mysticism treat ecstasy or
samadhi as a temporary alteration in consciousness occurring
spontaneously or brought about by various means. For some
of them it is a state akin to seizure or epilepsy which settles
periodically on the brain. Mircea Eliade calls it the 'cataleptic
state.' The symptoms displayed by some mystics seem to
corroborate this view. In some cases there is a close
concordance in externals between ecstasy and an epileptic
seizure or, as it were, a sudden spasm of the brain. There is
absolutely no awareness of the biological factors involved in
the condition which shows a varied pattern in different
individuals.

PERENNIAL ECSTASY

The most serious lacunae in the current knowledge about
mystical ecstasy, especially in the West, is about the fact that
mystical consciousness can be a perennial feature of human
life. The individual blessed with this gift does not fall into a
trance or enter into *samadhi* to experience an expansion of
the Self and unity with Universal Consciousness, but can stay

in that condition day and night while busily engaged in the various activities of the world. I know I am making a rather bold statement about a state which has seldom been encountered or commented upon by writers on mysticism in our time. But I am not alone in making this assertion. That mystical ecstasy or the *turiya* state can be a perennial feature of human consciousness has been known in India from the earliest times.

The author of Panchastavi makes a clear avowal of this extraordinary state in himself when he says (III.19): - "Free from all sense of dependence and dejection; neither seeking anything from anybody nor deceiving anybody, nor servile to anybody, I clothe myself in fine garments, partake of sweet foods and have for my consort a woman of my choice (enjoy all legitimate pleasures of life) because Thou, O Goddess, the fulfiller of all desires (in the form of Kula) are blooming in my heart." Abhinava Gupta, the famous Shaiva philosopher, makes a similar assertion about himself when he says, "It is Shiva Himself, of unimpeded Will and pellucid consciousness who is ever sparkling in my heart. It is His highest Shakti Herself that is ever playing on the edge of my senses. The entire world gleams as the wondrous light of pure 'I'-consciousness. Indeed, I know not what the sound 'world' is supposed to refer to."[29] The projection of inner light, kindled by Kundalini, lends the wondrous gleaming appearance to the outer world so beautifully described in this verse. It is the inner luminosity which shows one infinite Ocean of Consciousness pervading the Universe.

This is how Shankaracharya describes the same extraordinary state: - "That kind of mental function which cognizes only the identity of the Self and Brahman, purified of all adjuncts, which is free from all duality, and which is concerned only with pure Intelligence is called Illumination. He who has this perfectly steady is called a man of steady illumination." Again: - "He who, even having his mind merged in Brahman, is nevertheless quite alert, but free, at the same time, from the characteristics of the waking state (i.e. for whom the world has ceased to be an objective reality) and whose realization is free from desires, is accepted as a man liberated in life."[30]

The Indian school of Rasayana (Alchemy) aims at the transubstantiation of the body to make the condition of perennial ecstasy or *Jivan-mukta* possible while the individual is still alive. Rasayana is also a disguised form of Tantric sadhana. Rasa or mercury refers to the reproductive energy instrumental in the liberation of the soul and prolongation of life. Rasa is said to be the seed of Shiva and Abra the ovum of Gauri that is Shakti. It is through the combination of these two substances that immortality is attained. From this very definition it is clear that the phenomenon of the awakening of Kundalini is indicated. *Rasarnava,* a well-known work on Rasayana, describes the state of *Jivan-mukta* thus:

> "The light of pure intelligence shines forth into certain men of holy vision.
> Which, seated between the two eyebrows, illuminates the universe, like fire, or lightning, or the sun:
> Perfect beatitude, unalloyed, absolute, the essence whereof is luminousness, undifferentiated,
> From which all troubles are fallen away, knowable, tranquil, self-recognized.
> Fixing the internal organ upon that, seeing the whole universe manifested, made of pure intelligence,
> The aspirant even in this life attains to the absolute, his bondage to works annulled."[31]

The state of perennial union with universal consciousness is described in the commentary on *Pratyabhijna Hridayam* thus:- "On the attainment of the bliss of consciousness, i.e. on the attainment of 'Samavasha' (contemplative experience of unity-consciousness in which the entire universe is experienced as identical with the Self), there is firmness in the consciousness of identity with chit (mind) in body, pleasure, etc., even when they are experienced like coverings, i.e. there is lasting experience of unity-consciousness with chit (mind) in 'Vuytthana' (everyday normal experience). That firmness of consciousness of identity with chit is Jivan-mukta, i.e., Liberation of one who is still alive." The commentator adds the following words from Vasugupta's *Spandakarika* to illustrate and support his own statement: - "He who knows thus (i.e., as described before this verse in *Spandakarika*) and regards the whole world as a play (of the divine) being ever united (with Universal Consciousness) is without doubt liberated even while alive."[32]

It is clear from the passages reproduced above that the phenomenon of perennial ecstasy stands precisely defined in the Indian manuals on Yoga and Higher Consciousness and, in fact, is the ultimate target of all forms of Yoga. This puts an entirely new complexion on mystical ecstasy for the reason that if a perpetual state of transformed consciousness is possible, it means that the temporary interludes indicate but the sudden or gradual onset of a sublime condition which, in special cases, can become the lifelong, normal endowment of a human being.

This is then the aim of Yoga and the message of Panchastavi — the release of the soul from the domination of matter, the thraldom of senses and the prison of flesh to gain its sovereign, deathless estate while still alive. What temptation of flesh or treasure of the earth can even remotely match this surpassing, perennial experience of unbounded, eternal Life? What earthly Kingdom can ever attain the limitless proportions of Cosmic Consciousness? This is the reason why all through the past the sages of India classed perennial ecstasy as the supreme prize attainable through human life. This is the basic aim of all religions and faiths of mankind: this elevation of human consciousness to another dimension in which the spirit lives in the fleshy tabernacle conscious of its divinity, treating embodied life as but a single act of a Drama, conceived, directed and played by one Eternal Being, a Ray of whose splendor shines in him.

This is how Panchastavi (II.16) describes this Cosmic role of Universal Consciousness (Shiva): - "O Centralizing Power: It is when, of Thy own choice, Thou bringest the appropriate Gunas (the three qualities of Prakriti or matter) into fullness, then only does God Shiva, the sole Creator of the three worlds, become the Stage-Manager of the Cosmic Drama of existence." The era of triumphs over the forces of nature that followed the Renaissance in Europe has created an unwarranted spirit of arrogance among the empiricists and thinkers of our time that the dominion of life can be taken over by force in the same way. Such an attitude appears incredible when it is recollected that all these great triumphs sprang from the mind, about which we still know extremely little. This mind, in its turn, depends for its sanity and acumen on the play of subliminal forces, working in the body, over which we have no control at all. Then who are we to arrogate to ourselves the position of supremacy which we do not actually possess?

All this progress of which we are so proud is the outcome of the same leap forward that occurred in the life and career of some nations of the past, the Egyptians, Indo-Aryans, Greeks and the rest, that made them ascendant for a time, to be eclipsed again by other nations that could steal a march over them. This rise and fall of nations and all the achievements and the march of progress that occurred through it, have all been due to a collective activation of Kundalini, the sublime Evolutionary Energy in the race. That this has been recognized is clear from this verse (V.17): - "Sages call Thee the Mother of the Universe, the Fount of Talent and Wisdom, the Beginning (of creation), the Established Doctrine, Perception, the Harmonizing Energy, Spiritual Lore, the Preceptor, the Tradition, Humility, the Precept, the Authority, Final Liberation, the Highest Superhuman Power, the Supreme Secret, the Method, the (whole of) Knowledge and by other such names."

The answer to the riddle that baffles modern historians and thinkers was known to this unknown author in the dark ages of the past. The Power responsible for all our temporal and spiritual triumphs and all our intellectual advances is Kundalini. Is it a matter for wonder then that Shakti is devoutly worshiped by multitudes in India as the bestower of all the gifts that have contributed to the progress and welfare of mankind and all that is good, beautiful, noble, and chaste in man? The tragedy is that there is a deplorable lack of knowledge about this mighty architect of human destiny among the learned of our day. They do not know that there is an untapped source of mind-energy in the organic frame of man and that the highest luminaries and the greatest artists of the race, unknown to themselves, drew their inspiration from this hidden fount. The tragedy becomes even greater when it is seen what a poor picture of Yoga and Kundalini is presented to the uninformed but earnest, seeking crowds all over the earth by professionals who do not know what they are talking about.

The condition of lasting ecstasy with certain clearly defined characteristics, about which there is unanimity of opinion among the Indian authorities, in spite of variations in the interpretations, raises sundry issues of extreme importance which demand clarification. The features common to the condition are: 1) inward music and light, 2) a feeling of expansion in which consciousness assumes a cosmic proportion, 3) spontaneous happiness, welling up from within, 4) a sense of kinship to or identity with an infinite sovereign entity, beyond comprehension, 5) the mirage-like appearance of the objective world, 6) conviction of immortality, 7) a sense of highly extended knowledge, 8) extrasensory experiences and the rest.

For a transient experience of this nature, embodying all these characteristics, a host of explanations can be provided and they have been furnished by some of the modern writers on the subject. But a permanent condition, persisting in wakefulness, dream and deep sleep is not so easy to explain. Even if *samadhi* or ecstasy is held to be an encounter with God, Brahman, Allah, Ishvara or Shiva, the constant vision of the Deity before the inner eye of the experiencer, through all the varying moods and states of the mind, can only be explained on the grounds that a new channel of perception has come into operation or that another window of the soul has been opened for the glorious sight.

Faced with the question of how to explain the condition, modern psychology will most probably come up with the solution that the state is due to pathological causes, with grandiose delusions — a form of insanity that still remains to be classified. The resemblance of some of these characteristics to the symptoms noticed in some categories of the insane would fortify the presumptions. Withdrawal from the real world and entry into an imaginary world of one's own creation, which is such a marked feature of psychosis, would at once point to the identity of causes for the condition. But insanity is still an unsolved enigma of mental science. The Freudian and Jungian hypotheses which ascribed the condition to purely psychic causes are no longer accepted and a revolt has set in among the younger ranks. The latest investigations show that some forms of psychosis trace out definite pathways in the brain, which show that the malady has a somatic base.

Where this investigation will lead it is hard to say at present. But if insanity has a somatic origin, in the still unfathomed organic depths of the cerebrospinal system, and perennial ecstasy is also a form of insanity, it means that the same somatic alteration which, in the case of psychosis, becomes the cause of mental distortion, fear, anxiety, violence or abnormal behavior, in the case of perennial ecstasy gives rise to a state of mind which is the *summum-bonum* of all that one can wish for on this earth.

Even admitting that the condition is only delusive or imaginary, if such a blissful and creative state can become a lasting feature of one's consciousness, persisting through thick and thin, as schizophrenia does in the reverse direction, what more can a mortal desire in life? What can then compare with God-intoxication or the inebriation of Cosmic Consciousness? People resort to alcohol and drugs for self-transcendence, for a momentary escape from the harsh realities of everyday life and, on return to normalcy, have to pay a price for the short-lived release. What can then measure up to the fortune of one who is perennially lifted up from the narrow groove of normal human life into regions of everlasting glory, life and joy?

A permanent transformation of consciousness, lending a new meaning to life and leading to a new vision of the Universe, providing an unfamiliar ground for the intellect, may continue to remain a subject of controversy and debate until the number of visionaries of this class is large enough to furnish incontestable evidence for the condition. Until that time contemplatives of the perennial category will continue to be dubbed as insane by some and as Divine incarnations by others. The irony is that nature selects the vessels for this surpassing grace at her own choice, leaving the elite in other departments of life to wonder at the causes that lead to it. This is what Emerson tries to convey in these lines:

> O, when I am safe in my sylvan home,
> I tread on the pride of Greece and Rome;
> And when I am stretched beneath the pines,
> Where the evening star so holy shines,
> I laugh at the lore and the pride of man,
> At the sophist schools, and the learned clan;
> For what are they all, in their high conceit,
> When man in the bush with God may meet?

KUNDALINI AS THE IDEAL OF BEAUTY

The repeated reference to the charming contours of the
Goddess, for one brought up in the puritanical tradition of
any religion, must seem out of place in a work like
Panchastavi, venerated almost as a scripture. There are
frequent allusions to Her large, massive or bulging breasts,
Her lotus-like lovely bewitching eyes, Her beautiful waist, Her
lovely form like the orb of the moon and to Her other
seductive charms. Saundarya Lahari is even more prolific in
the description of Her beauty. Most of the sixty-two verses
comprising the Wave of Beauty are devoted to the meticulous
description of Her charms with all the power of the author's
poetic genius.

Every feature and every limb of the Goddess is seductively
depicted. Her eyes, soft with love, ringed with feather-like
eyelashes cause disturbance in the profound mental placidity
of Shiva. The arched pair of ridges (between Her eyes and
ears) has the grace of the bow of the flower-arrowed God of
Love. Her lips are of the color of coral, disclosing two
beautiful rows of teeth, Her tongue is the color of japa flower,
Her voice is melodious, Her chin is matchless, raised often
by Lord Shiva to implant a kiss. Her hands are like lotus dyed
red, with lustrous fingernails, Her arms are like creepers, Her
breasts like containers, chiseled out of ruby, and filled with
nectar.

Her beautiful waist has three folds, though slender yet
supporting the two breasts so large that they burst the
garment covering their sides and rub against the armpits.
Her hips are broad and heavy, Her thighs are like the trunks
of lordly elephants, Her knees rounded and Her feet
ravishingly beautiful. The poet sums up Her overall beauty
in one stanza at the end: - "The transcendent Aruna, Shiva's
grace incarnate, curly in Her hair, artless in Her gentle smile,
Shirisha-like in Her frame, hard like stone in the region of
Her breasts, extremely thin in Her waist, and prodigious in

the region of Her hips, excels in Her glory for the welfare of the world."

But why should Panchastavi dwell so ardently on the beauty of the Goddess and Saundarya Lahari enter into such meticulous detail about Her bewitching and entrancing charms? The answer to this lies in the very names assigned to the two sections of the latter work, to wit the Wave of Bliss and the Wave of Beauty. Bliss and Beauty are the two most prominent attributes of Shakti or Kundalini. Bliss and Beauty are also the two most outstanding features of Shiva-Consciousness. The entrancing lustre in the head of the yogi, covering everything he perceives with a mantle of light, permeated with a concentrated joy which surpasses every pleasure of the earth, bubbling up from the deepest depths of his being, transforms the normal human consciousness into an ocean of life, love and happiness that is impossible to describe. The inner man is changed. His consciousness itself now becomes the paragon of beauty, grace, melody, love, happiness, and peace. The animal passions are refined and calmed and the passion for all that is beautiful, harmonious and good becomes a dominating feature of life.

The love for harmony, music, beauty, art and poetry is peculiar to human beings. There is no aesthetic sense as such in animals. Where there is evidence of a predisposition of this kind in beasts or birds, as for instance in the lure of a beautiful color or gorgeous plumage or music in the cry of a mate, it is the outcome of a strictly bound instinctual response in which individual choice has no place at all. The evolution of the aesthetic sense in mankind has been proceeding for many thousands of years. We find evidence for it in the beautiful cave drawings, tattooing, wearing of plumes, and ornaments and in the use of other aides to beauty, according to their own peculiar tastes, by both men and women among primitive populations of the remotest times of which any record is available.

Judged according to the standards of our own day, the gulf between the aesthetic sense of the savage and the highly refined taste of the cultured populations of our time is very wide indeed. On the ethical side also the distance covered is enormous. From the evidence available, the inference is clear that cannibalism and human sacrifice were rampant among the primitive populations of the past. The abhorrence with which we view these practices now, from a long distance of time, is a clear index of the change that has occurred in the ethical standards of man. Constant pursuit of beauty and goodness and the continued elevation of ethical values are the two essential ingredients of a progressive evolution of the race.

> "If then beauty is the cause of good," says Plato, "then the good would be brought into existence by beauty, and it would appear that we devote ourselves to the pursuit of wisdom and of all other beautiful things for the reason that their product and offspring — the good — is worthy of devotion and from our explorations it looks as though beauty is metaphorically a kind of father of good." [33]

The state of absorption resulting from the contemplation of a beautiful object is well known. A lover never tires of drinking in the beauty of the beloved and may remain rapt in observing every feature, every contour, every limb, every word and every gesture of the desired person. Beautiful landscapes, dulcet music, pleasing odors, harmonious colors, charming faces and figures, superb masterpieces of art — all have an alluring and absorbing effect on the human mind. Reflection on an ugly, repulsive or obnoxious object can never lead to those states of sublime absorption in which the soul, in a condition of withdrawal from sensory impressions, contemplates itself. This is the reason why, for the devotees of Krishna or Rama, Vishnu or Shiva, the Gods are imagined as personifications of manly beauty, bodily strength and superhuman prowess.

The same holds true for the worshipers of Shakti also. She becomes the embodiment of feminine beauty, symmetry and grace. With the intensity of concentration and repeated practice, Her exquisite face and figure become familiar objects to the contemplative, leading to states of complete absorption in which only the seer and the object seen remain. Properly directed, alert meditative states of the mind exercise a stimulating effect on the mechanism of Kundalini. This is the reason why there is repeated mention in the manuals on Yoga and the Bhagavad Gita not to allow the mind to wander or to sink into reveries. The aim of the disciplines is to make higher consciousness an everyday waking feature of human life and not turn it into a visionary experience possible only in sleep-like mental states.

The use of flowers, music, lights and incense at the time of worship or the beauty in design and the grandeur of places of worship are all designed by their cumulative influence to heighten the effect of worship or prayer offered or meditation done in such surroundings. The subject will be dealt with in more detail elsewhere. Suffice it to say here that the ultimate aim of all worship, prayer, Yoga or any other religious discipline is to reach that sublime state of Union or Mystical Consciousness which is the radiating center of all that is pure, true, beautiful and harmonious in the Universe. This is the reason for the idea expressed by Abhinava Gupta in the *Tantraloka* that "the state of homogeneity produced in the mind through the absorbing interest of pleasurable sensations of sight, sound and touch leads one to the realization of the ultimate motionless nature of the Self, and the bliss that is derived from such experience is but a playful manifestation of the blissful nature of the Ultimate Being."[34]

This is the reason why our author, looking at the issue from another plane of consciousness, has not hesitated to delineate the superb charms of the Goddess. For the devotees of Shakti, the contemplation of beauty must be cultivated with the purest objective of reversing the direction of the reproductive mechanism, utilizing the precious energy not for momentary libidinous pleasure but for the much more elevating and much more entrancing transformation of the brain. The consciousness of the devotee himself then becomes the seat of a bliss which excels by far all the pleasures derived from the senses and even the ravishing transport experienced in the play of love.

"Great men who, with their minds bereft of impurity and illusion," says Saundarya Lahari, "look on Thy Kala (i.e., the Chandra-Kala when Kundalini enters the Sushumna) slender as a streak of lightning, of the essence of the Sun, Moon and Fire and abiding in the great forest of lotuses, standing far above even the six lotuses (chakras), derive a flood of infinite Bliss."

The repeated allusion to large and heavy breasts has another esoteric significance also. Female breasts are the receptacles of milk on which the human infant is nourished. Their large and massive size indicates a generous supply of the nourishing beverage. In the evolutionary scale the human adult of today is still an infant that has to grow to maturity with the attainment of Cosmic Consciousness. In this process of growth, that may take aeons to accomplish, he is to be fed on the ambrosial stream supplied by Kundalini to enhance the capacity of the brain. This nectarean substance, which floods the cranium in a lavish measure on the arousal of the power, is symbolically compared to milk.

The traditional representation showing Lord Vishnu reclining on Shesha-naga, floating on an ocean of milk, is a symbolic rendering of this concept. The body is an ocean of milk in which the floating Serpent of Kundalini extracts the life essences from all the tissues and organs to feed the stream which, when it flows downward, leads to reproduction and, when upward, to the evolution of the brain. It is in this sense that Shakti is addressed as Mother, with large, well-filled breasts designed to raise the human child to the stature of a Cosmic Conscious Being.

THE MAGNETIC POWER OF THE ILLUMINATI

In a number of verses, repeated reference is made by our author to the irresistible fascination exercised by the accomplished *sadhakas*, blessed by the Shakti, on the members of the fair sex who come in contact with them. "Lovely women, tormented by the fire of love, succumb to these men of concentrated minds. On them ceaselessly center the looks of charming ladies made restless by the arrows of Cupid." "Beautiful-eyed maidens casting away their modesty run after them and they become the objects of undivided attention, in the abode of Cupid, on the part of youthful maidens smitten with love." "Even if ugly they appear like the mind-alluring God of Love in the eyes of youthful damsels with large well-formed hips." With these and other telling phrases the author draws attention to the erotic aspect of the transformation effected by an awakened Kundalini.

At another place (III.5) he adds: - " 'I wish to drink him with my eyes,' 'I wish to touch his limbs with mine,' 'I wish to absorb him into myself.' Such are thoughts that cross the minds of youthful maidens in regard to the accomplished devotees of the Goddess when sitting in their company." Saundarya Lahari goes a step further to say: - "Damsels in hundreds with their locks disheveled, their sarees flying off their figures, their girdles bursting asunder with force, their silk garments slipping down, run after a decrepit, ugly and impotent man, who falls within the range of Thy side glances." This acquisition of a power of fascination is mentioned again and again in some of the Tantras and books on Shakti Shastra. According to Yoga-tattva Upanishad, Hatha-Yoga secures such personal beauty to the yogi that all women would desire him, but they have to be resisted. All these colorful and, at places, highly exaggerated statements are not without a hard core of truth. They refer to a profound psychological factor which forms the basis of attraction between the male and the female in the play of love. We still do not know what causes work and what magnetic waves pass between a couple intensely drawn to each other in the bond of erotic desire or what makes complete strangers take a sudden liking to each other.

The lion's mane and the gorgeous feathers of a peacock are alluring sexual characteristics provided by nature to draw the members of the opposite sex to the copulative act. A thousand different devices are used by nature to fulfil the supreme purpose of propagation. A high forehead, broad shoulders, an athletic figure and high intellectual or artistic gifts in men, beauty, grace and symmetry of face and figure, modesty, sweetness and gentleness in disposition, in the case of women, are some of the alluring features that not unoften exercise their sway in the intercourse of love between men and women in different parts of the world.

It is a well-observed fact that famous leaders, dictators, eloquent speakers, champion athletes, great actors, musicians, painters, as also well-known authors and even reputed saints draw crowds of admirers and adorers of the opposite sex. This is a phenomenon which has been witnessed all through the past and will continue to be witnessed in future also for it is an essential adjunct to the evolutionary dynamics of the human race. Still unidentified, mysterious forces work in the subconscious depths of human beings to create eugenic preferences and tastes helpful to evolution. But our lack of knowledge, adverse social barriers, impetuosity of youth and many other man-made factors stand in the way.

The statements made in Panchastavi, Saundarya Lahari and other works on Kundalini definitely refer to these hidden forces which create the ferment in the psychological depths of human beings. The ascent of Kundalini into the *sahasrara* has the potentiality to transform an average human being into a Cosmic Conscious sage, a genius of the highest order or a prophetic seer with highly-developed psychic gifts, full of vigor and charm. It is, therefore, no wonder if he becomes an object of admiration and love to members of the opposite sex who come within the circle of his influence.

These verses in Panchastavi and other allied works are only intended to emphasize the fact that, with the ascent of Kundalini into the brain, the adept attains a stature among mortals that even gods would envy. Beauty, health, lofty traits of character, higher intellectual and artistic gifts, and eloquence, with a magnetic personality, are the priceless boons attainable with the discipline. What is there then to belie the statement that accomplished yogis of this calibre would excite the interest and admiration of the womenfolk susceptible to their influence?

Examples of mass fascination exercised by great generals, popular leaders and extraordinary men of talent are still fresh in our memory. Napoleon Bonaparte and Adolf Hitler are but two known examples of this kind. The genius of Voltaire made even kings and aristocrats stand in awe of him. All these are cases of a naturally active Kundalini about which the individuals themselves had no knowledge at all. To what god-like stature voluntary arousal of the mighty Power, when its still undisclosed secrets are known, can raise the future recipients of the favor it is not possible even to imagine at present.

It is to this total transformation of personality, raising man to the stature of a superman, that Panchastavi (III.3) refers in the subjoined verse: - "O Goddess, before him, who even once humbly completely prostrates himself before Thee, emperors bow down from his very birth, the crests of their diadems laid trembling at his shining footstool. He who worships Thee is worshiped by celestials. He who sings Thy praises is praised far and wide. He who meditates on Thee becomes the object of fond attention on the part of beauteous damsels smitten with love." *Karpuradi Stotra* expresses the same idea in verse 22 thus: — "Numbers of women with large eyes, like those of the antelope, impatient for his love, ever follow him. Even the king becomes subject to his control. He becomes like unto Kubera (God of Wealth) himself. An enemy fears him as if he were a prison. Living in continuous bliss, the devotee is liberated when yet living, and is never again reborn."[35]

Erotic desire is a most essential factor in the unfoldment of the Drama of terrestrial life. Animals on land, birds in the air and fish in the ocean submit to it. Form, figure, features, colors, sounds, odors, signs and signals, all are used by nature to bring about the union of the sexes for this great purpose. The continuation of the human race, with all her great achievements, has been entirely due to the operation of this mighty urge. A forcible distortion, inhibition or extinction of the powerful impulse cannot but lead to distortion, decline or extinction of the race. For nature's plan of evolution it is absolutely necessary that the amatory impulse should continue to work to create more and more evolved specimens of humanity. Atrophy or extinction of the instinct implies a violation of the law of evolution and a negation of the Will of God.

It is idle to expect that an extended knowledge of the power reservoir of Kundalini can lift all the race to a higher dimension of consciousness within a foreseeable period of time. On the other hand, it is wiser to assume that the transition will take ages to accomplish. Both before and after the transition, gradations in the mental, physical and spiritual stature of individuals will continue to exist. With the climb of each step of the ladder, the number of highly evolved persons must show a progressive increase. It is not only in the achievement of higher ethical standards or superior intellectual talent, but also in the attainment of greater beauty, charm and longevity for the body that the evolutionary change will manifest itself.

It is safe to presume that the highest products of the process will exercise their power and cast their magnetic influence over the crowds among whom they live. The attraction felt by the other sex towards the prodigies of this class, to conform to the instinctive hunger for more evolved, ideal offspring, will continue to be a natural feature of human life as it is now. It is to these profound instinctive impulses in the human mind to which the verses refer. No man-made barriers or cultural prejudices can ever stand against the overpowering might of the evolutionary impulses. The institution of marriage and the play of erotic passion will always be subservient to the dictates of this irrepressible urge. The ideal forms of wedlock in which the ethical, erotic and eugenic demands will find fulfillment, in keeping with the overall purpose of evolution, have still to be determined.

From a distance of more than one thousand years, Panchastavi beckons the present-day war-torn, divided mankind to the glowing vision of a new world. Not the madding, shrieking world of giant machines, nor the diabolic world of magic, sorcery and supernatural power, nor the pleasure-crazy world of vice, crime and violence, but a world of harmony, beauty, peace and happiness, existing both within and without. Civilizations rose and fell without translating this glorious vision into actuality because ignorance of the physical laws of the Universe stood in the way of a better understanding of the laws of the spiritual world. Unhealthy asceticism in the field of religion, unbridled power in the hands of a few in that of politics, extremes of want and opulence in the social realm, and dogma in the sphere of knowledge combined to keep mankind fettered to ways of life antagonistic to the manifestation of the Divinity within.

The Divine side of the Universe, by too much stress on the material side alone, will always remain hidden from the sight of science unless this stubborn attitude registers a change. No power on earth and no achievement of the intellect can ever succeed in placing forever the god over the brute in man. The shift from good to evil and from evil to good will continue like a giant see-saw, lifting mankind up for a while to plenty and undisturbed peace and then plunging her down into the abyss of war, suffering and want. Were the Riddle of the Universe so easy to read that the puny human intellect could find the answer, it would reduce the Creator of this, for the human mind, unimaginable world, to the position of only a magnified human being. But continued penetration into the Mysteries of Creation for millions of years to come would not exhaust the infinite mine of wonders that shall continue to excite the curiosity of mankind.

The paramount importance of the research on Kundalini lies in this: that the very first successful experiment would reveal the hidden possibilities of spiritual transformation existing in the human frame, and the unbounded world of consciousness which this transformation can open to view. This experience alone can subdue the otherwise unyielding pride of the intellect. It is only when the dormant life forces in the body stir to activity to raise the perceptive powers of the mind that the illusion created by the senses fades to bring into view the glorious world of consciousness. This is what the author of Panchastavi has in mind when he says (V.1): - "O Mother of the Universe, Thou shinest as the moon to dispel the darkness, dread and fever of embodied life. All these followers of different creeds, in dark about Thy real nature, disputing with each other, stumbling and sinking deeper into the web of Thy illusion, helpless to save themselves, go to destruction. But we (Thy devotees), bowing to Thee, seek Thy protection, O Sovereign of the worlds."

It is only the inner transformation that can change for the better the outer environment of mankind. The animal chooses or creates its environment according to the demand of its instinct. Man creates his environment according to the dictates and tendencies of his intellect, but without long experience he can never be sure about the soundness of his choice. All the social and political orders ever formed have been only the reflections of the inner working of the minds of those who created them. Revolutions occurred whenever an attempt was made to superimpose a newly thought-of pattern over the one already in vogue. The change worked for the better when the good element predominated in the minds that devised the new pattern. The intellect was equally at work both before and after the change. But what makes the intellect more prone to good in one case and more prone to evil in the other, we do not know. This is the secret of Kundalini.

It is the predominance of the noble or divine element (*sattva*) in the leading intellects that alone can bring about a wholesome change in the affairs of man. The modern world, modeled on the blueprint designed by science, is proving a shrieking failure because the determining factor behind the intellect is still hidden from the eyes of the empiricists. The giant productions of technology, which overawe with their complexity and performance, are but the creations of an extremely subtle, invisible stuff, i.e., the mind which, in an individual, seems too weak for such a gigantic role. But we never suspect that there can be even subtler entities behind the mind that can make its giant creations either instruments of welfare or engines of mass destruction. It is, in ignoring the decisive part played by this determining factor behind the mind, that the greatest error of modern knowledge lies.

Without taking a lesson from the experience of the vanished cultures of the past, preserved in the religious literature of all mankind, to determine what disciplines and ways of life are necessary to bring about the predominance of the *sattvic* (divine) element in its mental constitution, humanity will continue to pay forfeit for the unpredictable errors of the intellect. It is only by upraising the divine that the brute can be vanquished. This cosmic Truth is represented symbolically in the saga of war between Mahishasura and the Goddess Durga (Kundalini) in which the former is killed. This has been mentioned to show what all-important, perennial Truths are embodied in the allegoric myths and stories contained in the Shakti Shastras current in India.

The Shakti Shastras and, in fact, all the ancient scriptural lore of mankind contain the living germs of a great discovery that alone can help science to bring about the glorious transformation of which we dream. But then material science itself will have to yield its pedestal to the now emergent Super-science of the Soul. It is Divinity itself that has come to live on earth in the guise of man. We are all Rays of light from an eternal Sun that is the life of all that exists in the Universe and the breath of all that breathes in any part of space. All the mineral and organic resources, so liberally provided by nature, are for the delectation of this immortal being to enable him to live and grow to the stature ordained by nature in his case. The instrument for his enjoyment of all the healthy pleasures of human life and also of his release from embodiment and illusion is Kundalini.

This is the great secret unfolded by Panchastavi when it says (III.15): - "O, Thou slayer of Asuras (demons), what sorrow (that can afflict human beings) is there which cannot be ended by keeping Thy remembrance constantly in one's mind? What is (the height of) fame, O Thou blooming lotus of Kula (the manifested world or Tantric system of worship) that cannot be attained by (singing) Thy praises? What Siddhi (perfection or psychic power) is there, O Thou adored one of the Deities, that cannot be gained by Thy worship and what Yoga is there that cannot be achieved by centering the mind in Thee?" This refers to the glorious future of emancipated mankind — legitimate enjoyment of all the healthy pleasures of earth — love, beauty, adventure, bodily comfort, food, drink, health, longevity and, at the same time, constant awareness of the Divinity and the immortal nature of the soul within. It is towards the realization of this idyllic dream that mankind, both in war and peace, laboriously inches its way up the steep ascent.

References

1. *Shankar Digvijaya* (XVI, 54-80)
2. Radhakrishnan, Sarvepalli, *Introduction to Bhagavad Gita*, G. Allan and Unwin, London, 1963
3. Krishna, Gopi, *Panchastavi* (XIX-XX), Central Institute for Kundalini Research, Srinagar, 1975.
4. Carrel, Alexis, *Man the Unknown*, Penguin Books, New York, 1975.
5. Wheeler, Sir Mortimer, *Indus Valley Civilization and Beyond*, Thames and Hudson, London, 1966.
6. Colebrook, Henry, *Miscellaneous Essays*, W.H. Allen and Company, London, 1837.
7. Goethe, Johanne W. VOII, *Wisdom and Experience*
8. *New Scientist*, October 1975, London.
9. Burt, Sir Cyril, *Psychology and Psychical Experience*, Wiley, New York, 1975
10. Murphy, Gardner, *Challegne of Psychical Research: Primer of Parapsychology*, Harper and Row, London, 1971.
11. James,William, *TheVarieties of Religious Experience*, New American Library of World Literature, New York, 1938.
12. Plotinus, *Enneads* (VI 9.5), Heinemann, London, 1966-67.
13. Gould, Stephen Jay, "A Threat to Darwinism", *Natural History*, December, 1975.
14. Penfield, Dr. Wilder, *Harpers Magazine*, December, 1975.

15. Sperry, Dr. Roger W., *Science of the Mind*, December, 1975.129
16. *Times of India*, Bombay, August 1, 1976.
17. Campbell, Joseph, "Seven Levels of Consciousness", *Psychology Today*, December, 1975.

18. Nicholson, Reynold A., *Rumi — Poet and Mystic*, Allen and Unwin, London, 1950.

19. Sagan, Dr. Carl, *New Yorker Magazine*, September, 1975.

20. Zimmer, Heinrich, *Philosophies of India*, Routledge, Kegan and Paul, London, 1951.

21. Russell, Bertrand, *Religion and Science*, Oxford University Press, Oxford, 1935.

22. Plotinus, *Enneads* (VI 9.3), Heinemann, London, 1966-67.

23. Shankaracharya, Vivekachudemani, Advaita Ashrama, Calcutta, 1970.

24. Kaul, Jaya Lal, *Lal Ded*.

25. Aiyer, K.N., *Laghu-Yoga Vasishtha*.

26. Wood roffe, Sir John (Arthur Avalon), *The Serpent Power*, Ganesh and Company, Madras, 1964.

27. Kaul, Jaya Lal, *Lal Ded*.

28. Freud, Sigmund, *The Future of an Illusion*, Hogarth Press, London, 1962

29. Singh, Jaideva, *Pratyabhijna-Hridayam*, Motilal Banarsidas, Delhi, 1962.

30. Shankaracharya, *Vivekachudemani* (427 & 429), Advaita Ashrama, Calcutta, 1970.

31. Acharya, Madhava, *Sarva-Darshana Sangraha*, Kegan, Paul, Trench, Trubner and Company, London, 1961.

32. Singh, Jaideva, *Pratyabhijna-Hridayam*, (16), Motilal Banarsidas, Delhi, 1962.

33. Plato, *Greater Hippias*.

34. Dasgupta, Shashibhusan, *Obscure Religious Cults*, Luzac and Company, London, 1969.

35. Woodroffe, Sir John, (Arthur Avalon), *Karpuradi Stotra*, Luzac and Company, London, 1922.

Panchastavi

FIRST CANTO

M ay the Goddess Tripura, who is of the nature of light and sound, shining in the forehead like the lustrous bow of Indra (i.e. the rainbow) in the crown of the head like the luminous white shine of the moon, and in the heart like the never-setting splendorous sun — may She, by means of the three mighty syllables 'Aim', 'Klim', and 'Sauh', speedily destroy all our impurities.

1.

We, Thy devotees, always meditate upon the vowel in Thy first syllable (Aim) resembling the fine first shoot of maiden-hair (a kind of fern) just beginning to sprout which itself is of the shape of Kundalini always engaged in the work of creation (of the universe). Realizing Thee in this form, man does not touch the womb of a mother again (i.e. is not reborn in this world).

2.

O giver of Boons! Whoever even on seeing an astounding phenomenon utters, out of wonder or fear, the syllable 'Ai', though without the dot (.) of the original 'Aim', upon him, too, O Goddess, Thy grace descends and from his lotus-like mouth flow ambrosial expressions full of nectar (i.e. he becomes an eloquent speaker).

3.

Eternal Goddess, whoever realizes that the seed syllable in Thy Mantra 'Klim' which is 'Kamaraja' (giver of complete fulfillment) is the same as Thy first syllable 'Aim' (bestower of Buddhi or wisdom), he, too, becomes the recipient of Thy grace and even though dull-witted, becomes enlightened or wise. (For this reason) at every festival held in the memory of Satya-Tapas-Rishi, the Brahmins begin their recitations manifestly with 'Aim' instead of the usual 'Aum'.

4.

From my heart I bow before Thy third seed syllable (Sauh) which is lustrous like the moon and whose power has been realized by the wise in instantaneously causing flow of speech. Just as the Wadwa (submarine) fire is effective in drying up the backwaters of Saraswati River, so is the (Sauh) syllable effective in destroying ignorance and granting Siddhi (success in spiritual striving) without even the practice of Yoga.

5.

Each one of these three faultless syllables 'Aim', 'Klim', and 'Sauh' with or without consonants, in combination with other letters or with letters written separately (in the normal order) or in the reverse order, but contemplated in whatever manner, or recited silently, with whatever wish in mind, each one of these, O Goddess, grants instantly all those desires of Thy devotees.

6.

O Mother, how can they attain Seership, who do not learn to meditate on Thee, holding a rosary in Thy right and the book (of wisdom) in Thy left hand, with one soft hand raised to grant boons and (the other) to dispel fear, shining like white camphor and Kumuda flowers, looking with bewitching glances from Thy lovely eyes (shaped) like the petal of a full-blown lotus.

7.

O Saraswati (Kundalini as the Goddess of Learning), verily there pours out from the mouths of those devotees who contemplate Thy entrancing resplendence, spotless like unto a bunch of white lotuses, irradiating the brain and dwelling in the forehead, akin to a stream of ambrosia, an uninterrupted forceful flow of words, clear and full of deep meaning, like the milky and wavy lustre of the river of Gods (the Ganges).

8.

Lovely women, tormented by the fires of Cupid, with eyes like those of frightened young deer, in every way succumb to the fascination of those men of concentrated minds, O Goddess, who even for a moment meditate on Thy lustre (of crimson hue) covering the sky with clouds of vermilion dust and submerging the earth in folds of molten lac.

9.

Blooming prosperity, as unstable as the earflaps of an excited elephant, bewitched stays for long in the abode of those (devotees) who, even for a moment, with one-pointed mind meditate on Thee, (adorned) with bright gold earrings and bracelets and with a golden waist-band worn round Thy waist.

10.

With the crescent moon adorning Thy matted and braided hair, wearing a garland of human skulls, clothed in red attire like the blossom of the Bandhuka flower, seated on a corpse, having four arms, three eyes, large and elevated breasts and the middle of Thy body marked by three deep lines, the followers of the Heroic Path meditate on Thy figure to realize Thy true nature.

11.

Born of a very humble family of Kshatriyas with a modest pedigree, it was by virtue of the favor earned through bowing at Thy lotus feet, that Shri Vatsaraja rose to the Emperorship of the whole earth and won such surpassing glory that crowds of demigods offered worship to his feet.

12.

O Goddess Chandi: How can they be born as emperors invested with regal insignia in the form of sceptre, goad, discus, axe, arrow, with the sign of fish on their lotus-like bright hands, when those hands have not worked ceaselessly and gotten pricked in the process by myriads of thorns while collecting Bilva leaves for the purpose of worshiping Thee?

13.

O Goddess Tripura: Pervading the visible and invisible worlds, whatsoever by the Siddhi (psychic gift) for which Thy devotees of stable intellect pray for (be they) Brahmins, Kshatriyas, Vaishas or others, who propitiate Thee with (the offerings of) milk, clarified butter, honey, and wine in the ritual of worship, they undoubtedly, freed from all obstructions, gain fulfillment (of all the boons prayed for).

14.

Thou art the source of all sounds in the universe. Thou art also the origin of all speech and (hence) art called by the name (of the Goddess of Speech). Vishnu (creator), Indra (the lord of the elements) and others (other divine Beings) issue from Thee and at the end of the world-cycle verily are absorbed into Thee. It is in that (highest) form, full of majesty which is beyond conception, that Thou are sung as Para-Shakti (Supreme Energy).

15.

The three Deities (Brahma, Vishnu and Shiva), the three fires (sacrificial, household and crematory), the three Shaktis (desire, knowledge and action), the three sounds (tenor, low and medium), the three worlds (this world, the nether and the upper world), the three-syllabled Gayatri (Energy of Buddhi), junction of three rivers (Ganga, Jamuna and Saraswati), the three Brahmas (Man, Energy and Shiva), and the three castes (Brahmin, Kshatriya and Vaisha) — in fact all these and others that are modeled in three ways (i.e. which are threefold in nature), truly follow in principle Thy blessed appellation O Goddess, Tripura.

16.

In royal families with the recitation of Thy name as Lakshmi, on the field of battle with the recitation of Thy name as Jaya, in routes infested with tigers, lions, etc., wild elephants and serpents with the recitation of Khemankari, on dreary and impassable mountain paths with recitation of Shavri, in the dread of evil spirits, ghosts, goblins and jackals, etc., with recitation of Maha-Bhairavi, amidst terrors with the recitation of Tripura, and in flooded waters with the recitation of Thy name as Tara, (Thy devotees) find release from calamities.

17.

Thou art Maya (the illusory power of the Creator), Thou art Kundalini, Energy of action and bliss, Thou art Kali (creative, preservative and destructive energy), the nectar-raining moon, the garland of letters (i.e. learning), the daughter of Matang Rishi, bestower of highest victory, the Energy of Shiva and the darling of Shankara, Thou art three-eyed benefactress Durga, the fount of speech, Tripura (commanding the three channels — Ida, Pingala and Sushumna), Bhairavi (the dispeller of fear), Hrimkari (of the form of Hrimkara), gross and subtle both, Mother of the universe and immaculate destroyer of duality (existing in the human mind).

18.

O Goddess Tripura: By inserting a vowel, from AA to EE at the beginning and end in prescribed order to consonants from ka to ksha, singly or in combination with two or three, those extremely subtle names of Thine that are verily formed in this way, O consort of Bhairava (Lord Shiva) and which number more than twenty thousand, I offer my salutations to all of them.

19.

This hymn of praise to the Goddess (Saraswati) — the patron of learning — should be reflected upon by the wise and sage by their penetrating minds fixed on Her and on nothing other than Her, knowing that Tripura is all, to understand that in the very first stanza, in the first, second and third lines, the number of words, their prescribed order and the method for the compounding of right mantras, according to the established tradition, have been plainly described in detail.

20.

Why think whether what is expressed in this stotra is correctly rendered or not? He who is devoted to Thee will surely read this hymn (and reflect upon it). Because despite the knowledge of my own little worth, I, too, composed this hymn verily by dint of my faith and persistent striving with my whole being.

21.

SECOND CANTO

Thy beautiful lotus foot, O Mother, on which God Indra, in bliss, (at the victory gained over the Asuras through Thy favor) placed a necklace of pearls, the same foot which forcefully pressed on the head of Mahishasura (the chief of the Asuras) and the sweet jingling of whose anklet bewitches the mind (of Thy devotees), may the same foot be the cause of victory to me.

1.

O Mother of the universe, Goddess Tripura, the sphere of Thy surpassing beauty, like the Kalpa Vriksha (wish-fulfilling tree), becomes the means of granting the boon of sovereignty of the three worlds and the talents of a poet (to Thy devotees), in the same way as the full moon brings a host of Kumuda flowers to bloom. (Hence) these salutations made to Thee, O Goddess, become the cause of victory (to Thy worshipers).

2.

O Goddess, even the very wise Brihaspati (the high-priest of the celestials) and the Devas (shining ones), fail in their efforts to sing Thy praises. Therefore, how can an inherently dull-witted person like me stand anywhere in praising Thee, who art the spouse of (Lord Shiva), the destroyer of demon Tripurasura?

3.

O Mother: Even so (despite my inadequacy) my passionate devotion unto Thy lotus feet makes me somewhat articulate in singing Thy praise which is the means to overcome the acute fever of the world (i.e. its suffering and misery) and act as a helmsman to ferry one across this ocean of sorrow.

4.

O Bhawani (Shiva's consort): Thou is the Creator as well as the Preserver of the worlds. At the same time, Thou art alert towards their destruction, when the time is ripe. Thou dost destroy delusions though hiding Thy real self. All this, Thy sport, is triumphant, though bewildering in its way.

5.

O Gauri: Spotless like a newly-opened lotus petal, upon whomsoever out of even a small measure of grace Thou dost cast a kind glance, on him (Thy devotee) ceaselessly center the looks of charming ladies made restless by the arrows of Cupid.

6.

It was through the Grace emanating from the dust particles on Thy lotus feet that the eminent Udayana (a terrestrial lord), whose footstool even the demi-gods (Vidyadharas) reverently kissed, obtained the sovereignty of the whole world.

7.

O Bhawani (spouse of Shiva): with flowers from Kalpa-Vriksha (the tree of paradise which fulfills all desires), the demi-gods perform their unique worship of Thee and sing songs full of exhilarating, extremely sweet, enrapturing music, playing these songs on subtle Vina (a kind of musical instrument) without cessation in their cavernous abodes on Mount Sumeru (the Golden Mount).

8.

O Goddess, in the effort to bring Lakshmi (the Goddess of Wealth) under one's control and in the aim to attract lovely women to oneself, as also in lighting the lamp which dispels the thick darkness of delusion, the infallible Mantra to achieve success is the Grace emanating from Thy feet.

9.

O Goddess, the luminous beams, issuing from the gem-like nails of Thy feet, as bright as the lustre of ever-fresh pearls, cause untold happiness (to Thy devotees). The same beams adorn, like a cluster of flowers, the head at the place where the hair is parted of the consorts of gods, when they bow devoutly before Thee (in worship).

10.

The splendor, which shines like the cool rays of the moon in the head, like the colored beams of a rainbow in the middle of the forehead and which kisses the heart chakra like a tongue of fire, that splendor, verily, is Thy own glorious Form, O Mother.

11.

He (Thy devotee), who perceives Thy (lustrous) form, like the white rays of the full moon, and as the primeval fount of all articulation in his head, that devotee, O Goddess, acquires the gift of limitless flow of words, rich with the ambrosia of sweetness and beauty of expression.

12.

O Goddess Tripura: He who perceives (during meditation) even for a moment, the sky colored with a coat of vermilion dust and the earth steeped in the red juice of lac with Thy glory, beautiful-eyed maidens, O Goddess, casting away their modesty, run after him.

13.

O Mother: He who contemplates Thee, even for an instant, like the fine fibre stretching out from the juice of lac, that devotee of noble virtues becomes the object of undivided attention, in the abode of Cupid, on the part of youthful maidens tormented by love.

14.

O Goddess: The Jewel that shines as the moon in the sky-like ocean of mind, that which is the primeval Being, the mentor of the celestials and demons both, and that which is the left half of the destroyer of Andhaka (a demon), i.e. Lord Shiva, Thou art verily all that (O Kundalini).

15.

O Centralizing Power: It is when, of Thy own choice, Thou bringest the appropriate Gunas (the three qualities of Prakriti or matter) into fullness, then only does God Shiva, the sole Creator of the three worlds, become the Stage-Manager of the Cosmic Drama of existence.

16.

O Rudrani (Shakti): Those (devotees of Thine) who meditate on Thy unique appearance, wearing a rosary of reddish corals (Rudraksha), luminous like the morning sun, they are adored by youthful women with lovely eyes who, drawing close to them, wind their soft and creeper-like tender arms round their neck with all their force.

17.

Whoever meditates upon Thy imperishable form, crimson like a fully opened pomegranate blossom, and pays homage to Thee as Kamadeva (Cupid), he himself, even if ugly, becomes the mind-alluring God of Love in the eyes of youthful damsels (adorned) with large, well-formed hips.

18.

O Daughter of Himalaya (spotless like snow): The devotee who, with a pure heart, meditates on Thy stainless glory, like a cluster of moonbeams, O Beauteous One, Thou dost soon bless him with unlimited power of faultless expression (genius) in a matter of days.

19.

O Goddess: He who, after having gained the power to raise the Vayu (prana) from Muladhara into the heart, perceives Thee in the form of a fine fibre of lotus, dyed in vermilion, he becomes the object of adoration of Siddhas (perfected beings) and Sadhyas (Gods).

20.

O Bhawani: those devotees, who see Thee clearly like the crescent of the moon, shining in the forehead, lighting from its depths the sky of the mind, these wise men soon become seers and Thou grantest all desires to these discerning souls full of faith.

21.

O Goddess: Thy devotees in their eulogies call Thee as all-pervading, benevolent, as Kundalini (the Serpent Power), as the fulfiller of desires, as Goddess of Fortune, as Goddess of sixty-four Arts, as wearing a garland, as beauty incarnate, invincible, as one granting victory and success, and as the consort of Lord Shiva.

22.

O Mother: Those devotees who meditate upon Thee as existing in the halo of the sun, red like unto fresh lac, to them always become submissive (out of intense love) gazelle-eyed beauties, their bosoms pierced through and through by the arrows of Cupid.

23.

O Goddess Tripura: shining with the lustre of burnished Gold, heated in fire, may Thou cleanse me and make Thou cut down the dense forest of sins clinging to me through many lives. May my remembrance of Thee instantly break asunder the fetters that bind my suffering self to the prisonhouse of the body.

24.

O Goddess of Dissolution! Adorned with eyes beautiful like the petals of a lotus, Thy lotus feet command the homage of multitudes. Roaming King-Swan-like the lake of mind of pure-hearted devotees, Thou destroyest all evils threatening those who take refuge in Thee.

25.

Only a few, taking refuge in the dust of Thy lotus feet, became great poets, pure in heart, of great wisdom and noble deeds and won to fame which resounded in the three worlds, stainless like the moon, silk, milk, or snow.

26.

O Goddess: May my eyes ardently seek to visualize Thy form, may both my ears ever long to listen to descriptions of Thy countless virtues, may my mind ever be engaged in Thy remembrance, may my voice always be raised in Thy praises, may my two hands ever be busy in actively worshiping Thy feet. (In short), may my zeal for worshiping Thee never diminish in any way.

27.

I make obeisance to Thee, O Goddess Tripura, who actest like the warm glow of the sun in bringing the lotus-cluster of one's intense desire for higher knowledge to bloom, who when worshiped in six ways, (i.e. with the five senses and the mind) dost become the sporting arena of the lion of wisdom ready to kill the elephant of delusion.

28.

O Thou Goddess Tripura Sundari (supreme beauty of the three worlds), who art worshiped by Ganesha and Vatuka (Bhairava), having pleasurable connection with the Eros, having for Thy exalted seat Lord Shiva Himself, armed with the arrows of Cupid and adorned with the flowers of the God of Love, with Brahma, Vishnu and Mahesh forming the members of Thy family, residing in the midst of the forest of Kadamba trees. May thou, O Tripura, grant protection to us.

29.

Whoever, without remission, reads this auspicious stotra of the Goddess or listens to it reaches the fulfillment of all his

desires. He is worshiped even by kings and becomes intensely
dear to beautiful women with gazelle eyes.

30.

O Goddess of speech: Mistress of the three worlds, Creatrix
of the universe, pervading both within and without, adored
by Brahma (the Creator), Vishnu (the Preserver), Rudra (the
Destroyer), Indra (the Lord of Elements), Chandra (the
moon), the sun, Kumara and Ganesha (sons of Shiva and
Parvati) and by Agni (God of Fire), my obeisance to Thee.

31.

THIRD CANTO

O Goddess Parvati, consort of the three-eyed Shiva, Daughter
of Himalaya, Immaculate, Eternal Mother of the three
worlds, Shivay (benefactress), Sharvani (Durga), Tripuray
(trilateral), Mridhani (transporting), Vardhey (bestower of
boons), Rudrani (of frightful aspect), Katyayani (clothed in
red), Bhimay (terrible), Bhairavi (consort of Bhairava),
Chandi (the fierce), Sharvari (alternately dark and pale in
complexion), Kalay (Irenic), Kalakheye (the annihilator of
time and the destroyer of Death), Shoolini (the wielder of
the spear), may Thou, (O Goddess) grant us, Thy devotees,
bent in contemplation at Thy feet, protection from the
afflictions which beset us on every side.

1.

Distraught like one possessed, swooning as if with the effect
of poison, or like those drowned in affliction due to
separation (from their beloveds), intoxicated, lost to the
sense of their own self, damsels with lovely eyebrows dwell
constantly in their minds on those fortunate devotees who,

with undivided attention, free from distractions, worship
Thee, O daughter of Himalaya (Kundalini).

2.

O Goddess: before him, who even once humbly completely
prostrates himself before Thee, emperors bow down from his
very birth, the crests of their diadems laid trembling at his
shining footstool. He who worships Thee is worshiped by
celestials. He who sings Thy praises is praised far and wide.
He who meditates on Thee becomes the object of fond
attention on the part of beauteous damsels smitten with
love.

3.

O Tripura! They, who meditate on Thee with their whole
being even for an instant, though lacking the fortune of
charm and youth, imprint their image on the exclusive
murals of the minds of entrancingly beautiful large-eyed
belles (i.e. are able to command the love of beautiful
women).

4.

What (sacrifice) is there, O Goddess, which youthful maidens
would not do for him, (Thy devotee) who cherishes Thee
in his heart? "I wish so much to drink him with my eyes (look
constantly at him)." "I wish to touch his limbs with mine." "I
wish to absorb him into myself or to enter into and be one
with him." Such are the thoughts that arise in their minds
(in regard to him), lost to all control over themselves.

5.

O Creatrix of the Three Worlds: Just as the word 'Ishvara'
(the lord) applies exclusively to the all-pervading Shiva, self-
existing and eternal, in the same way, O Goddess, the very
same word (Ishvari) applies to Thee also as Thou art the
'Shakti' or the potency of Lord Shiva. This being so, it is very

strange that Thou dost not, in Thy wrath, destroy the petty worldly afflictions which form a potent cause of hindrance to Thy devotees.

6.

O Bhawani (Goddess Parvati): Mortals who, with one-pointed mind, meditate on Thee, seated on a white, full-blown lotus, shining like a lamp brimful with oil, spotless as camphor or like the orb of the moon, soul-captivating and nectar-raining, they are set free from the miseries of existence (birth, death, etc.) and all calamities stay away from them.

7.

Those (devotees) who, in all humility and faith, meditate on Thee, dwelling in their minds on Thy form like the orb of the full moon, or a vast ocean of milk (heaving) with waves of elixir, resembling globes of concentrated nectar, (white) like snow, they (even though) afflicted by sorrows and calamities, attain to spiritual and temporal prosperity (by Thy Grace).

8.

Those who constantly think of Thee as being (perpetually) in motion (like the rise and fall of ocean waves) prone to create (and destroy) at Thy wish, tearing asunder the five knots, crimson like the newly-risen morning sun, drowning the alluring world into an enrapturing pink ocean of joy, they (O Goddess) occupy the minds of gazelle-eyed women (fond of them).

9.

Lovely, fawn-eyed belles intensely adore with their peerless lotus eyes, as if he were Kamadeva (the God of Love), him. O Bhawani, who ceaselessly dwells in his mind on Thee, resembling the fine fibre of a lotus stalk dyed in the sap of lac, (residing) in the Sushumna.

10.

Lustrous, like the moon, white like snow or like a Jessamine flower, wearing a garland of red Kadamb blossoms, hanging down to the soles of Thy feet, we worship Thee as the unmanifested source of speech (in the para form).

11.

Flawless, exceedingly sweet and beautiful, soul-enchanting, uninterrupted flow of words (speech) manifests itself on all sides in them (Thy devotees blessed by Thee with genius) who keep Thee, O Shakti (of Shiva), the destroyer of Kamadeva (God of Love), constantly in their mind, as shining with the stainless lustre of the moon in the head, seated on a gleaming lotus-throne, sparkling with the white glitter of snow, sprinkling nectar on the petals of the lotuses both in the Muladhara (the root-center at the base of the spine) and Brahma-randhra (the cavity of Brahma in the thousand petalled lotus in the head).

12.

O Goddess, meditated upon even once with one's whole being, what (goal) is there that you do not accomplish without the least difficulty? You bestow all wished-for chattels of enjoyment, destroy one's enemies, drive away calamities, subdue diseases of the body, burn away impurities, stamp out forcibly the suffering and sorrows of the mind, enhance happiness, and cure the pangs of separation (from near and dear ones).

13.

O, Thou beloved of the Three-eyed (Lord Shiva), whosoever meditates on Thee, recites Thy name, perceives Thee, thinks of Thee, follows after Thee, surrenders himself unto Thee, reflects on Thee, lauds Thee, takes shelter in Thee, worships Thee, or who with reverence, listens attentively to (the recitation) of Thy (divine) attributes, the Goddess Lakshmi (dispenser of spiritual and temporal wealth) never stays away

from his abode and victory (everywhere) runs in front of
him.

14.

O, Thou slayer of Asuras (demons), what sorrow (that can
afflict human beings) is there which cannot be ended by
keeping Thy remembrance constantly in one's mind? What
is (the height of) fame, O Thou blooming lotus of Kula (the
manifested world or Tantric system of worship) that cannot
be attained by (singing) Thy praises? What Siddhi (perfection
or psychic power) is there, O Thou adored one of the Deities,
that cannot be gained by Thy worship and what Yoga is there
that cannot be achieved by centering the mind in Thee?

15.

Thy constant remembrance, O Goddess, saves (from
destruction) those who have fallen into the inexorable jaws
of death, liberates those, O Kali, who are caught inextricably
in the thick noose of all-devouring time and (safely) ferries
across those, O Chandi (of fierce aspect), who are drowned
in the ocean of dreadful heinous sin.

16.

The specks of dust of Thy feet, as potent in effect as the
(magical) charms used to propitiate (bring under control)
Lakshmi (the Goddess of Wealth) remain ever victorious.
Those specks of dust, O Goddess, sticking to the foreheads
(of Thy devotees), when they bow down at Thy lotus feet (in
obeisance), can erase (even) the adverse writ of Fate
(otherwise ineffaceable).

17.

O you ignorant beings (sunk in worldly delusions), why do
(some of) you profitlessly torment your bodies by (extreme)
penance and austerity, and others impoverish themselves with
(the drain of) heavy payments for religious sacrifices (and

ceremonies)? If your devotion is unflinching, then serve the two feet of the immortal Goddess and (soon) auspicious Lakshmi (the Goddess of Wealth and prosperity), with a canopy of full-blown lotuses, will run in front of you.

18.

Free from all sense of dependence and dejection; neither seeking anything from anybody nor deceiving anybody, nor servile to anybody, I clothe myself in fine garments, partake of sweet foods and have for my consort a woman of my choice (enjoy all legitimate pleasures of life) because Thou, O Goddess, the fulfiller of all desires (in the form of Kula) are blooming in my heart.

19.

O thou, immaculate Goddess, bearer of the Cosmic sound, the beauteous Mistress of the Three Worlds (or the three states of waking, dream and dreamless slumber) to whatsoever extent, according to my capacity, I can recite Thy name or offer Thee worship, pray do accept that, O Parameshwari (Supreme Ruler of the universe).

20.

May all those striving for perfection attain to happiness, may all evil propensities of the wicked perish, may I attain to the Shambhavi state (oneness with Universal Consciousness) and may my Guru (spiritual preceptor) always remain well pleased with me.

21.

O Thou beauteous Mistress of the Three Worlds, the sight of Thee (darshana) washes away the sins (of Thy devotees), the recitation of Thy name destroys the fear of death and Thy worship drives away misfortune and pain.

22.

Adorned with the crescent of the Queen of the Night (the moon), in the hair on Thy head, and like a stream of nectar washing away the suffering of worldly existence, I make obeisance to Thee, O Bhawani (the Mistress of Creation).

23.

Whatever (omission) has occurred through me, due to my lack (of knowledge) of the Mantra, or of religious rites or of the prescribed methods (to perform them), for all that, out of compassion, pray forgive me, O Parameshwari (Supreme Ruler of the Universe).

24.

FOURTH CANTO

She whom the sages have called by the name of primeval Prakriti (nature), She whom the knowers of the essence of the Revealed Scriptures (Vedas) designate by the name of pure knowledge and She who as the half of Shankara (Lord Shiva) causes Him to manifest Himself, I, having no other shelter, take refuge in Her.

1.

When in singing Thy praises, even the beautiful hymns of the Vedas, which are revealed (i.e. have no mortal author), appear insipid, it is only the love overflowing in Thy heart, O Mother, which finds pleasure in this incoherent hymn of praise (composed) by a dullard like me.

2.

In the mind of fortunate devotees, O Mother, Thou dost manifest Thyself as the glowing sky (Super-Consciousness), as the Bindu (non-dimensional void), as Nada (the Cosmic sound), as the crescent of the moon, as the fount of expression (genius), as Mother, as the fount of Bliss and the Nectar of Jnana (supernal knowledge).

3.

O Mother, with hairs on their bodies standing on end, with tears streaming down from their eyes and with their voices quivering with emotion, those (devotees) who ceaselessly worship Thy feet in their heart, they are, indeed, blessed.

4.

Very rare indeed is the man (Thy devotee), O Mother Goddess, whose mouth, by dint of great austerity done, is always occupied in Thy praise, whose head ceaselessly bows before Thee and whose mind is always absorbed in Thy thought.

5.

O Goddess, rising from the cavity of Muladhara (the root-center at the base of the spine), piercing the six lotuses, like a flash of lightning, and then flowing from the moon into the immovable sky-like center (in the head), as a stream of Supreme Nectar, Thou then returnest (to Thy abode).

6.

O Goddess, from the time when on (an amorous) look from Thy bewitching eyes (Lord Shiva) revived the withered Kamadeva (Cupid who had been burnt by an angry glance from His Third Eye) to life, from that day, out of shame, Shiva verily keeps the Third Eye in His forehead closed.

7.

O Parvati (Daughter of Himalaya), One whose parentage and lineage are not known anywhere, who is a mendicant with a garland of skulls round his neck, naked, without any settled abode and without a second, how could anyone know this Shambu (Lord Shiva) before His auspicious conjugation with Thee (i.e. Thou art the cause of His manifestation).

8.

For One like Shiva, dressed in skins, His body besmeared with ash from (cremated) dead bodies, wandering for alms, dancing in the habitations of ghosts, and gathering hosts of earth-spirits round Himself, it is only Thy association with Him that lends charm to all these attributes.

9.

O Mother, it is only Thy creative aspect (benign look) which moderates the highly skillful, albeit fierce, 'Tandawa' dance of Shiva, whose weapon is the axe, and transforms it from world-destroying sport into the glory of creation.

10.

O Thou Benefactress, (even) for those seekers after salvation, whose actions are balanced and who take shelter in the favor of a guru, it is Thou, O Goddess, who, in a moment, breakest asunder the fetters (of karma) that bind them, and initiatest them into the secret teaching of the Shaiva Scriptures.

11.

One in whose heart Thou shinest like the star-studded dusk ornamented with pearls and glowing like fresh coral, he alone of all becomes the Kamadeva (God of Love) to beautiful Eyes of three worlds without using the five arrows (or the five-fold sensual allurements to captivate them).

12.

O Mother, Thou sovereign (fount) of Ambrosia, those (Thy devotees) who devoutly think of Thee as irradiating the three worlds with myriads of nectar-raining beams, verily pass across (the boundaries of) Time (or Death) which is extremely difficult even for Brahma and other exalted heavenly beings to cross, (i.e. they attain to Super-Consciousness beyond time and space or the fear of death).

13.

O Mother, the devotee who worships Thee in his mind, as holding a rosary of crystals in one of Thy hands, a noose, a book and a chalice in the other two and the fourth raised (in the gesture) to expound and teach, resplendent like the autumnal moon, and seated on lotuses, he becomes the foremost among all poets and logicians in the world.

14.

O Shavari, the wife of the hunter Shiva bearing the crest of peacock feathers on Thy head, with curly locks of soft, shining, deep brown hair, a rosary of red berries resting on Thy heavy breasts, in color like the evening sky, with a face like red coral and soft and tender hands, O Thou Shakti of Shankara (Shiva) I bow down before Thee.

15.

O Beauteous One, why did Thou barter half of Thy body (soft) like a fresh-born creeper, brought up with love, with the coarse half of Lord (Shiva) giving rise to banter on part of Thy female friends (the senses and the mind)? But, methinks, with only a gentle (mind alluring) smile on Thy part, they are (all) frozen into silence (i.e. they are hushed into immobility with the first glimpse of the glory of Kundalini).

16.

How strange it is, O Mother, that this ocean of illusion (i.e. this creation born of Maya) confusingly crowded with countless cosmic hosts like bubbles (on its surface), filled with waves of (countless) diverse kinds of affliction, with the submarine fire, generated by constant meditation on Thee, is destroyed in an instant (i.e. is dissolved into consciousness).

17.

O Bhagvati (Sovereign of the Universe), though in Thy transcendental aspect Thou art the daughter of Prajapati

(Lord of the Universe) also the serpentine Kundalini, dweller in the cavity of the heart, as also Katyayani (dressed in red), also Kamla (Lakshmi, the Goddess of Wealth) and Kalavati (the Goddess of Arts), in this way verily, like a dancing girl, Thou art seen in countless forms (and roles).

18.

O Empress of the World: Those blessed ones who inwardly experience Thy blissful aspect at the place known as Anahata (heart chakra) in the form of Nada (Cosmic sound — the source of all speech) express the ecstasy of this encounter with their hair standing on end (through the intensity of emotion) and tears (of joy) pouring from their eyes.

19.

Thou art lustre in the moon, radiance in the sun, intelligence in man, force in the wind, taste in water, and heat in fire. Without Thee, (O Goddess), the whole universe would be devoid of its substance.

20.

Those starry hosts that roam the sky, this atmosphere which gives birth to water, this Shesha-naga (a mythical serpent) which supports the earth, the air which moves and this fire which shines bright with leaping flames, they all, O Mother, exist only by Thy command.

21.

O Thou Daughter of the Mountain (Himalaya), when Thou contractest Thyself (i.e. withdrawest Thyself into Thyself), then Thou art without name and form, beyond reason and language both (i.e. inaccessible to intellect and hence inexpressible in words). When Thou expandest Thyself (i.e. manifestest Thyself as nature) then it becomes easier to make a count of Thy names and forms.

22.

O Goddess, righteous men, who pay obeisance to Thee for (a life) of fulfillment (both temporal and spiritual) find thousands of Lakshmis (Goddesses of Wealth and Learning) obedient to their every sign (to every slight knitting of the brow), and pass long lives of enjoyment, sporting with mounds formed of myriads of Chintamani gems (Philosopher's stone that turns everything to gold or grants every desire) in gardens full of Kalpa trees (trees of Paradise which fulfill every wish).

23.

O Ruler of the Universe, just as the heat, caused by multitudinous rays of the sun is abated by the showers also brought about by him (i.e. the sun), in the same way, O Goddess, it is only Thou, who through Thy Grace alone art able to destroy all the suffering of existence which, too, is subservient to Thy will (i.e. caused by Thee).

24.

O Goddess, Thou art the Shakti (Power) of Shiva (the Creator), who has the moon on His forehead. Thou art His body, the senses, the mind, the intellect, the power of action and the doer of deeds. Thou art desire, rulership and also delusion. Thou art His refuge as also the veil that hides the reality. What is there which doth not spring from Thee?

25.

Thou art spoken of as inertia in earth, sustenance in water, incantations offered in fire, tranquility in air, supernal peace in ether. All the thirty-six Tattvas, (constituent elements of creation) that manifest the universe, are Thy own estate and yet Thou art far above them all, O Fond Mother!

26.

O Thou Refuge of the World, so long as Thy two lotus feet do not accept a place in one's heart, the complicated and tortuous polemical disputes caused by the varied thinking of the exponents of different cults and sects can never come to an end.

27.

O Parvati, those (yogis) who, making their mind the sovereign of all their senses, direct (the flow of) their Prana and Apana (flowing through the paths of the Deities and the Manes, i.e. the Right-side and the Left-side paths), through Thy path (in the middle i.e. Sushumna) they alone are able to take their seat on the heads of the five Karnas (Brahma, Vishnu, Rudra, Sada-Shiva and Ishvara, i.e., they become even greater than these Gods).

28.

O Goddess, even in Thy gross forms like that of earth, water, etc., a master of eloquence like Brahma has not been able to describe Thy glory. How dost Thou then, O Mother, put up with this (my poorly composed hymn of praise)?

29.

O Mother, those who meditate on Thee as the purifier of the six paths, blazing like millions of destructive fires, and flooding these worlds with the torrential rain of nectar, as also like a maiden in full youth with bulging breasts, Thou bring them fullness, and they thus become world-teachers.

30.

O Mother, some (of Thy devotees) call Thee as Supreme Knowledge, some as the encompassing atmosphere, some as (the fount of) bliss and some as Maya (the veil of illusion), while others see Thee as the Universe and still others in the form of a Guru (who is) limitless compassion personified.

31.

O Thou Mother of all the worlds, why speak further (about Thy attributes)? Our only prayer is (that) Thou may manifest Thyself to us in Thy supreme dark-blue aspect, like a host of blue waterlilies with curly, moist, glistening, tawny hair and with protruding breasts hanging down on Thy beautiful waist.

32.

FIFTH CANTO

O Mother of the Universe, Thou shinest as the moon to dispel the darkness, dread and fever of embodied life. All these followers of different creeds, in dark about Thy real nature, disputing with each other, stumbling and sinking deeper into the web of Thy illusion, helpless to save themselves, go to destruction. But we (Thy devotees), bowing to Thee, seek Thy protection, O Sovereign of the worlds.

1.

(O Goddess) who art beyond the reach of Speech and Logic, able by Thy own essence to awaken (Thy devotees) to the (inner) kingdom of Supreme Bliss (Shiva-Consciousness), shining all over with the lustre of the blue lotus, worthy of adoration even by the Supreme Deity, Shiva, bent with the weight of Thy large, heavy breasts, we make obeisance to Thy entrancing splendor which is beyond the grasp of mind and beyond the power of language to describe.

2.

With the necklace of the red seeds of the Ganja shrub hanging down (from Thy neck) in between Thy voluminous breasts, glistening with the oozing, tiny drops of sweat, resembling the brightness of the blue lotus, Thou, garbed as a huntress (Shavari), followed Shiva, clever in his role as a hunter, to afford protection to Arjuna. My obeisance to Thee again and again.

3.

Dialecticians, tearing out each other's hair in disputation are doomed to perish, (end in chaos), while the enlightened ones use methods replete with faith, devotion, love and humility. (For this reason) O Parvati, (Daughter of Himalaya), be gracious unto us, reveal Thyself unto us, grant us refuge as our minds, devoid of support, roll here and there (i.e. are confused) in this engulfing flood (of polemics).

4.

No human being can ever know, O Mother, when, how and where this (body of ours) will become food for dogs, for flocks of birds or for fire. Therefore, forsake forthwith Thy trust in this body and seek refuge in the Mother of the Universe.

5.

O Goddess, who hath no beginning and no end, although fully appreciative of Thy attachment to Non-Duality (bearing unalterable attachment to Lord Shiva) yet, full of love Thou didst join Thyself in wedlock to Shiva and although Thou art the progenitor of all creatures, yet Thou Thyself didst take Thy birth as the Daughter of Himalaya. This is the delightful aspect of Thy Grand Drama of Creation.

6.

O illustrious Goddess, some there are who declare Thee to be Real (perennially Existent). There are others who call Thee Unreal (Transitory). There still are other intelligent thinkers who proclaim Thee to be Real and Unreal both. (Apart from these), there are still other wise sages who hold that Thou art neither Real nor Unreal. O Goddess, O Thou

Consort of Shiva, all this is but the manifestation of Thy illusive power.

7.

With the brilliance of millions of flashes of lightning cutting Thy way through the six-knotted dense forest (the six chakras on the spinal axis), sprinkling nectar (on Thy way), Thou returnest to enter Thy abode (in the Muladhara). Shining with all the thirty-eight rays of light complete, luminous with Thy dark blue complexion and tawny hair, I make unceasing obeisance to this seldom-seen, unique phenomenon of Thine (an activated Kundalini in the process of Her ascent to Sahasrara and return back to Muladhara at the base of the spine).

8.

Located between the four-petalled and the six-petalled lotuses (Muladhara and Svadishthana), at the end of the cavity of pudenda (i.e. between the rectum and the genital organs), coiled three times, beaming with unbounded splendor, like that of sun, fire or lightning, Thou dost first pierce the six-petalled lotus (Svadishthana), then the ten-petalled (Manipura), then the twelve-petalled (Anahata), then the sixteen-petalled (Vishuddha), and then the two-petalled (Ajna chakra on Thy way to Brahma-randhra). O Parvati, (Daughter of Himalaya), our obeisance to Thee.

9.

O Thou Almighty weaver of illusions, some there are who declare Thee to be of the nature of Kula (the manifested universe compounded of thirty-six tattvas). Some other wise ones consider Thee to be Akula (unmanifested, i.e. beyond the objective world). Still others acclaim Thee to be Kula-Akula (manifested and unmanifested both), while some others believe Thee to be the Deity of Kaulas (the follower of the left-hand path). But there are still others, (in wisdom), above these four categories, who hold Thee to be unique and indescribable. How then (O Goddess) can we grasp Thy real nature with certainty?

10.

Shining with the brilliance of millions of suns at the time of Dissolution, with Thy splendor Thou burnest to ash the forest with the six routes (the world of illusion created by five senses and the mind) of those devotees whose heads remain bent at Thy lotus feet; making fully manifest (to them) the glory of the unparalleled Shiva with the effulgence of Thy lotus-like form, bent with the weight of breasts which, as the prowess of Shiva, is ever victorious.

11.

O Mother, Unknown and Unmoving before, entering the middle Path (Sushumna), Thou swallowest the pair, known as the Sun and the Moon, (Prana and Apana flowing in Pingala and Ida) and in the form of light and bliss reachest the uppermost center (Sahasrara) to be absorbed there. When arrived (there) Thou burnest to ash with the fire (of absorption) the elements (constituting the world and the body) which bind the incarnate soul. (In this way) the Jiva by Thy favor attains to the state of (all-pervading) formless Shiva.

12.

Those (devotees) who meditate constantly on Thee with Thy limbs dark-blue in color, like the Priyunga creeper, dressed in red, resembling its (unopened) buds, and Thy form bent with (the weight of) Thy two voluminous breasts, (bulging out) like massive bunches of its Pearl-like fruit, adorned with fully blossomed flowers, the bestower of all desires, like the wish-fulfilling creeper, they (those devotees, O Goddess) attain to the Chintamani state (all-desires-fulfilling gem) of Shiva Consciousness.

13.

It is Thou, O goddess, who dost lead the flowing nectarean stream of methodical (Yogic) discipline bearing the Supreme Nada (Cosmic Sound), of which the six-fold Tantras are the whirlpools, Mudras (special positions of the hands or the body) are the unsteady (mass of) foam, wearing countless shapes, Mantras are the endless series of waves, and the Deities (invoked during the practice) are the alligators, into the ever-fresh ambrosial ocean of Shiva Consciousness.

14.

O Mother, how great is Thy glory that even though swallowed up by earth, water, fire, air, mind, the sun and moon (i.e. though enveloped by all these elements in the embodied Jiva), in Thy superfine state of sky-like (expanded) Consciousness, not a trace of any of these enveloping sheaths is found there.

15.

O Mother, this whole creation of human beings, beasts, birds, and (demi) gods (comprising the three worlds) wallows in the depths of the ocean of existence, tossed up and down by countless waves caused by the three Gunas (Sattva, Rajas and Tamas). But one compassionate look of favor from Thee (O Goddess) on any one of the embodied creatures (human beings) can instantly grant him the supreme Bliss of Self-Realization.

16.

Sages call Thee the Mother of the Universe, the Fount of Talent and Wisdom, the Beginning (of creation), the Established Doctrine, Perception, the Harmonizing Energy, Spiritual Lore, the Preceptor, the Tradition, Humility, the Precept, the Authority, Final Liberation, the Highest Superhuman Power, the Supreme Secret, the Method, the (whole of) Knowledge and by other such names.

17.

With the cessation of (the impressions coming through the senses of) touch, sound, etc., and after that with the elimination of the circle of thought and thereafter at the quiescence of the entity (self), freed from the limitations imposed by the (aggregate of the series of) eight sounds (i.e. the world of name and form), through the grace of Shakti, yogis taste (the bliss of) the supreme condition of that readily recognizable, self-perceptive, profound plane of consciousness which is known as the Shiva State.

18.

O Thou, who wearest the form of Supreme Bliss, immeasurable sovereign Shakti (Power) of Lord Shiva, instinct with supernal knowledge and unlimited compassion, the Creatrix of all beings, the sustaining Base of the Supreme Abode, it is only Thy worshipers who remain (in eqipoise) whether in worldly life or when liberated (from it).

19.

Having absorbed the universe into the body (due to the shutting out of the stimuli coming from the senses), the body, too, in the heart (mind), the heart in the self (ego consciousness), the Bindu-sustained (i.e. non-dimensional) self also in the concentrated plane known as Nada (where the Cosmic Sound begins to be heard), that Nada also in the sphere of Supernal knowledge and that in the sovereign state of Supreme Bliss, (O Thou Goddess) who art of the form of the mighty sky (sky-like expanded consciousness) they (Thy devotees) who apprehend Thee (in this form) are ever victorious.

20.

O Thou, who art the Code of Conduct (in religious observances), the Repository of all Knowledge, fit to be comprehended, the Source of all Established Doctrines, the Author and the Quintessence of the Vedas, the Mine of

Wonders, the Origin of the Universe, the Controlling Power of Lord Shiva, the Springhead of all Morality, the Abode of Shiva-Consciousness and the Instrument of Unity with Him, O Mother, who art (inseparable from) Shiva, easily attainable through humility, bestow on us (the boon of) unparalleled devotion to Thee.

21.

O Mother, it was all through Thee, as the Shakti (Power) ever abiding in Shiva, that Shankara (Lord Shiva) was able to sever the head of Brahma (the Creator of the Universe) and use it as a (begging) bowl in His hand. Also, after transfixing Vishnu (the Preserver of the Universe) with His trident, was able to place Him as an ornament on His shoulder (i.e. to carry His body slung over His shoulder) and to adorn His own throat (with a blue mark) on swallowing the (halahal) poison (i.e. was able to resist the lethal effect of the terrible poison that rose from the Ocean when it was churned by the Devas and the Asuras).

22.

O Mother, O Parvati (Daughter of Himalaya), under the name Brahma Thou bringest the three worlds into existence, under that of Vishnu Thou sustainest them and in the guise of Rudra destroyest the same. Thou also assumest the state of Ishvara (the Sovereign Lord of all) and in the form of Sada-Shiva, breaking asunder the fetters (of Illusion), dost lead to blissful Shiva-Consciousness. Although one (in reality) with Thy own self-created modifications, Thou dost manifest Thyself in countless forms.

23.

Even holy sages, O Mother, who have completely purged their mind of worldly attachment, with their intellects overawed (by Thy splendor) are never able to gain the smallest bit of knowledge concerning Thee (i.e. art not able to understand Thy nature). How can the Upanishads, which form the crown of the Vedas, and which are essentially difficult (to understand) find a place at Thy extremely tender and delicate lotus feet, O Parvati (i.e. even they cannot comprehend Thy glory because of their essentially recondite nature).

24.

The righteous (knowers of Transcendental Truths) call Thee, O Goddess, as the Creeping Plant of Lightning (because of the serpentine, zigzag course She adopts while ascending through the spine), yet Everlasting and Infinite, as the River of Nectar, as the Lustre of the Moon without any spots, as Unfathomable Maya-Prakriti without the tangled knot of Gunas (Sattva, Rajas and Tamas), as Knowledge beyond Speech, as the Mother of the Unbounded Universe with firm, protuberant breasts, as Lakshmi (the Goddess of Prosperity) and with other such names.

25.

O Parvati (Daughter of Himalaya), this embodied conscious being (the average mortal) cognizant of his body, composed of earth, water and other elements, experiencing pleasure and pain, even though well-informed (in worldly matters), yet not versed in Thy disciplines is never able to rise above his egoistic body-consciousness.

26.

At the time when my father, mother, brother, wife, very loving friend, household, my own body, son, attendant and even wealth forsake me, at that time (of departure from this world) do'thou, O Moonshine-like infinitely Glorious Mother, out of compassion dispersing the (binding) darkness of ignorance, attachment and fear, instantly manifest Thyself unto me.

27.

O Thou Mother of all beings, verily Thou first took Thy birth as the Daughter of Daksha (Daksha Prajapati) and afterwards, discarding that defective association, Thou wert born as the Daughter of the King of Mountains (Himalaya). And, O Beginningless and Endless Sovereign of Creation, although as the Shakti (Power) of Shiva, inseparable from Him, yet Thou, with the bond of marriage, didst assume the relationship of His Spouse. Who can understand this, Thy amazing (mode of) behavior?

28.

The sun, moon, fire and other luminous bodies shine with but an extremely small fragment of Light (borrowed) from Thy infinite splendor. (Although) from Lord Shiva to the earth the whole universe (composed of thirty-six tattvas of which earth represents the first and Shiva the last Tattva) is contained in Thy thrice-folded form (as thrice-folded Kundalini possessing the three attributes of Sattva, Rajas and Tamas) yet how strange it is that Thou Thyself bloomest in the heart of a devotee.

29.

O Mother, that very Shambhu (Shiva) who perennially by virtue of Thee (His Shakti) is able to comprehend, by virtue of Thee is able to create, and by virtue of Thee is able to desire, when in the state of harmony (i.e. when not disturbed by this three-fold activity) attains to the sky-like Supreme State (of Universal Consciousness). In this manner, by discarding the creative or the illuminative state Thou dost sport with Him (i.e. change His state according to Thy pleasure). (O Goddess) why is it so?

30.

That which has gone before, that which is to come after, that which is within and that without, the unbounded and the limited, the most gross and the most subtle, the manifested and the unmanifested, the open and the secret, the near and the distant, being and non-being, in these and other forms Thou, (O Goddess), art perennially seen as the Universe. It is the movement (creative activity) born of Thee at Thy command which brings the (infinitely varied) Cosmos into being.

31.

Just as the rays of light rising from the sun, as the gleaming sparks rising from a fire, as the drops of spray formed by obstructed waves rising from the mighty ocean, (are reabsorbed in their source), in the same way, the multitude of elements rising and rising again with their own essential (constituent) groups are helplessly forced to fall back into stillness in Thee.

32.

Thou are Brahma (the Creator), Vishnu (the Preserver) and Thou art matter, the embodied Soul, ego-consciousness, the Moon, the Sun, Nature (of things), the Lord of Jains (Mahavira), the illumined sage (Buddha), sky, air, also Shiva and Shakti. By these different names, O Goddess, Thou art heard of and called by the righteous.

33.

The fortunate (seekers) who, by virtue of the Mercy inherent in Thy nature and (the favor of) a discerning preceptor, entering their own Path (Sushumna), are able to cleave the enshrouding darkness of the six routes (i.e. the illusory external world created by the five senses and the mind), at once know Thee directly unto the last day as their own (indwelling) illustrious Durga in the form of incomputable Compassion and Supreme bliss who maketh the body also auspicious, (so that it is able to sustain the flame of Super-Consciousness lit up by Thee).

34.

O Mighty Goddess, Thou art Shiva, Thou art Shakti, Thou the Established Doctrines, Thou the soul, Thou the initiation,

Thou this (manifested universe), Thou the Siddhis (psychic gifts), like Anima and the rest (i.e. all the eight Siddhis possible to yogis), Thou the aggregate of Gunas (Sattva, Rajas and Tamas), Thou knowledge and also ignorance. Thou (verily) art all and what is beyond it. What Tattva (element) there is (O Goddess) which is apart and different from Thee, we do not perceive.

35.

O Mother, even after attaining the excellent Shiva, as the gracious Preceptor and winning to the order of Shiva-Consciousness, at the end of the cycle of births, resulting from the cessation of Karma, earned in uncountable incarnations in the past I may, O Goddess, while wearing this body, spend the days of my life in communion with Thee, in singing Thy praises and in performing acts of worship to Thee.

36.

In that blooming lotus of six petals (Svadishthana) of which the Yoni (the place of generation) is known as the Karnika (arrow-like), and in the middle of that Yoni there is seen a Pedestal in the form of Aumkara (triangle), and in the interior of that (Pedestal) lies coiled (Kundalini), the Mother of all Creation, dark-blue in color, bent with the weight of Her two breasts, who is the object of unremitting devotion in my heart.

37.

O Thou Creatrix of the Three Worlds who, although (in reality) One, art yet (divided) in eight forms as the energy in earth, water, fire, air, ether, sun, moon and the performer of the sacrifice (the embodied Soul), bent with the weight of Thy bosom, yet still sustaining the Universe, may Thou protect me as that (Thy protection) is (in truth) indispensable (for me).

38.